MLA 9 Simplified: Easy Way Guide to MLA Handbook

Updated for the MLA 9th Edition Handbook

Student Citation Styles Series

Book 7, 1ˢᵗ Edition

Appearance Publishers
2021

MLA 9 Simplified: Easy Way Guide to MLA Handbook
Updated for the MLA 9th Edition Handbook

Student Citation Styles Series
Book 7, 1st Edition

"MLA 9 Simplified: Easy Way Guide to MLA Handbook" is specifically designed for students and professional writers to quickly learn updated MLA Style in a convenient and easy way.

With this guide, you will be able to format your paper according to the MLA style right away thanks to its easy-to-navigate structure and step-by-step guidelines on setting up research papers in MLA format.

Updated for the MLA 9th Edition Handbook, this guide offers general guidelines and multiple examples that allow writers: to cite most types of sources; to format title pages, running head, headings, lists, etc.; to learn more about in-text citations, quoting, paraphrasing; to create Works Cited list in MLA format; to use footnotes and endnotes; to format tables, figures, and examples, etc.

Includes MLA-formatted Sample Paper.

Learn more about quotation marks, italics, abbreviations, numbers, etc.

CONTENTS

FOREWORD...6

1.0 INTRODUCTION 7

2.0 IMPORTANT CHANGES IN THE 9TH EDITION 8
  Inclusive Language 8

3.0 GENERAL GUIDELINES.............. 11
  3.1 Paper Layout 11
  3.2 Running Head 12
  3.3 First Page (Title Page) 13
  3.4 Headings 14
    Level 1 15
    Level 2 15
    Level 3 15
    Level 4 15
    Level 5 15
  3.5 Text Styling 17
    Quotation Marks in Text 17
    Italics in Text 17
  3.6 Works Cited 18
  3.7 Tables, Figures, and Examples 19
    Tables 19
    Figures...20
    Examples 21
  3.8 Lists...22
    Integrated into Sentence.................22
    Set Vertically 23
  3.9 Numbers...................................25
    Number Ranges 25
    Dates 25
    Time 25
  3.10 Notes (Footnotes and Endnotes) 26
    General Format 26
    Content Notes.............................27
    Bibliographic Notes 27
  3.11 Abbreviations..........................28
    Most Common Academic Abbreviations.................28

4.0 IN-TEXT CITATIONS 29
  4.1 Introduction...............................29
  4.2 Formatting In-Text Citations 29
    Punctuation 30
    Pagination 31
      Sources without Page Numbers 32
      Commonly Studied Literature.............32
      Notes in Sources.........................33
      Time Stamps 33
  4.3 Titles of Sources........................34
    Shortening Titles 34
  4.4 Authors 35
    1 Author 35
    2 Authors 35
    3+ Authors 35
    Organization as Author.................36

2+ Authors with the Same Name...............36
2+ Works by the Same Author 37
2+ Sources for the Same Citation 37
Same Author and Same Title.................38
No Author 38
Multivolume Works 39
Scripture 39
Indirect Source 39
  4.5 Quotations and Paraphrases 40
    Paraphrases 40
    Quotations 40
      Short Quotations 41
      Long Quotations.........................42
    Making Changes to Quotations 44
      Omitting the Part of Quotation 44
      Adding to or Clarifying the Quotation.................44
      Adding Emphasis 45
      Fixing Errors 45
      Changing Syntax 45

5.0 WORKS CITED 46
  5.1 General Guidelines 46
  5.2 MLA Template of Core Elements 47
    1. Author 48
    2. Title of Source 49
    3. Title of Container.....................50
    4. Contributor..............................51
    5. Version....................................52
    6. Number....................................53
    7. Publisher 54
    8. Publication Date........................55
    9. Location 56
      DOI 56
      URL...56
    Supplemental (Optional) Elements.................57
    Complex Works 58
  5.3 Authors 59
    1 Author 59
    2 Authors 59
    3+ Authors 60
    Organization as Author.................60
    No Author 60
    Pseudonyms 61
    Online Author 61
    2+ Works by the Same Author 62
  5.4 Titles of Sources 63
    1. Capitalization 63
    2. Punctuation 64
    3. Styling....................................65

6.0 IN-TEXT CITATIONS / WORKS CITED EXAMPLES
....66
  6.1 General Format 66
  6.2 Books 66
    1 Author 66
    2 Authors 66

3+ Authors 67
Organization as Author 67
Unknown Author 67
Edited 68
Translated..68
Chapter in a Book 69
Multivolume Set..69
2+ Publishers..69
E-Book 69
Audiobook..69
6.3 Articles in Scholarly Journals 70
Printed Journal 70
Online Journal 70
Special Issue..70
In a Database (with a DOI) 71
In a Database (with a URL) 71
PDF of Online Journal 71
6.4 Articles in Periodicals..............................72
Printed Article in Newspaper 72
Online Article in Newspaper 72
Printed Article in Magazine 73
Online Article in Magazine 73
Review 73
6.5 Other Printed Works 74
Published Interview 74
Conference Proceedings..............................74
Lecture, Talk, and Speech 74
Entry in Dictionary 75
Entry in Encyclopedia 75
Dissertation and Theses 75
Short Story / Essay 75
Brochure..76
Letter 76
Report 76
Executive Summary 76
Poem 77
Play 77
Scripture..77
Bible 77
6.6 Websites 78
Webpage 78
Wikipedia 78
Entire Website..78
Facebook 79
Instagram..79
Twitter 79
Blog Post 79
6.7 Audiovisual Works 80
YouTube 80
TED Talk 80
Film..80
TV Series 81
Music Album 81
Song 81
Podcast 81
Painting (in Museum) 82
Photograph (Online)..................................82
Sculpture 82
Slides 83
Table 83
Chart..83
Map 83
6.8 Legal Works 84
Government Publication 84
Resolution of International Convention....................84
US Supreme Court Decision 84
US Code 85
US Public Law 85
Federal Bill 85
Executive Order 86
State Senate Bill 86
Treaty 86
Constitution..86
6.9 Personal Communications 87
Personal Communication 87
Personal Interview 87
Letter 87
E-mail 87
Classroom Material....................................87

7.0 MLA SAMPLE PAPER 88

SOURCES 97

MORE FROM THE AUTHOR................................98

Thank you for the purchase!

Do you enjoy reading?

As a thank-you, we are happy to give you some free goodies…

Get Your

FREE

Extra

follow the link:

https://appearancepublishers.wordpress.com/mla-9-simplified/

to get your FREE extra

Your support is much appreciated and we are looking forward to hearing your thoughts on your purchase!

FOREWORD

MLA (Modern Language Association)

This student guide reflects the newest version of the *MLA Handbook (9th edition)*, which was released in April, 2021.

This student guide will assist you to learn how to use the Modern Language Association (MLA) Style for references and citations. Revised according to the 9th edition of the *MLA Handbook*, this guide is offering guidelines and examples on:

- **Formatting paper**:
  - Title Page
  - Running Head
  - Headings
  - Lists
  - Abbreviations
- **In-text citations**:
  - Quotations
  - Paraphrases
- **Works Cited list**
- **Notes**:
  - Endnotes
  - Footnotes
- **Tables, figures, and examples**

including:

- **MLA sample paper**

This guide will address the vast majority of questions about using MLA style correctly. However, if you are working on a complex document or if you require in-depth information on a specific area of MLA Style, please consult the MLA Handbook (9th edition) for more details.

If you are a student, consult with your professor to find out what style your discipline requires prior to choosing MLA Style for formatting your paper.

Keep in mind: your instructor is the final authority on how to format your paper correctly.

Appearance Publishers
2021

1.0 INTRODUCTION

Referencing is acknowledging the copyrights of resources used in your academic writing, which gives all necessary information to identify the work cited within the text.

MLA (*Modern Language Association*) Style provides clear guidelines for writing research papers regardless of the chosen subject in most disciplines in the humanities.

MLA goals are:
- To provide standards for documentation and citation,
- To spread adoption of those standards among students and writers,
- To instruct students and writers on those standards.

Give credit to the sources that you have used and referred to in your research:
1.   Briefly acknowledge sources with in-text citations,
2.   Include complete descriptions of sources in the Works Cited list.

Therefore, **2 main segments** in the MLA referencing style are:
1.   In-text citations and
2.   Their corresponding entries in the list of Works Cited.

This guide assists writers in avoiding plagiarism and formatting paper according to MLA.

2.0 IMPORTANT CHANGES IN THE 9TH EDITION

The MLA Handbook (9th edition) improves the explanation of how to format research papers according to MLA style:

- Formatting title pages (including group projects),
- Formatting headings,
- Formatting lists,
- Formatting endnotes and footnotes,
- Formatting tables, figures, and examples
- Using italics and quotation marks in the text,
- Using inclusive language,
- Formatting in-text citations:
  - How to cite sources with 2 and 3+ authors:
    - New guidelines suggest including both first names and surnames when mentioning the authors for the first time in the text for sources with 2 authors.
    - New guidelines suggest using "and colleagues" instead of "et al." in the text for sources with 3 and more authors.
  - How to format block quotes.
  - How to cite prose, poems, and drama.
  - How to cite notes from sources in parenthetical citations.
  - How to shorten titles in parenthetical citations.
  - How to style titles in parenthetical citations.
- Formatting Works Cited entries:
  - How to use core elements on the MLA template in details:
    - **Author:** New guidelines on how to include and format pseudonyms.
    - **Title of Source:** New guidelines on how to provide cite sources with no titles, how to cite introduction parts, how to cite scriptures, etc.
    - **Publication Date:** New guidelines on how to format seasons for the dates.
    - **Location:** New guidelines on how to include URLs and format DOIs ("https://" protocol is now optional for URLs and is required for all DOIs).
    - **Supplemental Elements:** New guidelines on how to provide additional information.

Inclusive Language

To bring writing in line with best modern practices, MLA encourages choosing inclusive language to be respectful to sensitive individuals and group identities by avoiding bias with regard to:

- Age,
- Gender,
- Sexual orientation,
- Race,
- Ethnic identity
- Religion, and
- Social status.

- Refer to **relevant** identities:

INCORRECT:	**Man**-made…
CORRECT:	**Human**-made…

INCORRECT:	Men…
CORRECT:	People… Human being… Humanity…

- Remain **accurate** when using labels:

INCORRECT:	The **Muslims**…
CORRECT:	**Shia Muslims**…

INCORRECT:	**Buddhists** believe…
CORRECT:	A **Buddhist belief** is…

- **Avoid** using **pronouns that exclude or generalize**:

INCORRECT:	**We** are **all** concerned about what it is happening…
CORRECT:	**Most people** are concerned about what it is happening …

- Use **"they" as a singular pronoun** for a person whose gender is irrelevant or unknown:

INCORRECT:	When a person spends much time reading books, **his or her** skills become…
CORRECT:	When a person spends much time reading books, **their** skills become…

INCORRECT:	There is a candidate for our position, A. F. Johnson, we would meet and talk to **him or her** in person…
CORRECT:	There is a candidate for our position, A. F. Johnson, we would meet and talk to **them** in person…

- Remain **thoughtful** about capitalization, styling, and use of italics and quotation marks:

INCORRECT:	"homosexual"
CORRECT:	homosexual

- Choose **respectful terms** with regard to your subject:
    - Choose person-first language or identity-first language depending on the preferences of individuals or groups:

Person-first language:	A person **with asthma**…
Identity-first language:	An **asthmatic** person…

- **Avoid judging** person's experience **in a negative way***:
    - Use a dictionary to double-check for offensive terms:

INCORRECT:	**Victim of**… **Stricken with**… She **suffers from** anxiety…
CORRECT:	He has **muscular dystrophy**… She is diagnosed with **an anxiety disorder**…

*Hints: 1. To directly quote an offensive term from the source, use a note in your text to indicate it.

    2. To avoid reproducing an offensive term from the source in full, add a dash after the first letter of a term.

3.0 GENERAL GUIDELINES

3.1 Paper Layout

Margins:
- Leave 1-inch margins on all sides.

Text:
- Choose an easily readable font where the plain text contrasts with the italics:
  - *For example:* Times New Roman.
- Set the font between 11pt. and 13pt.
- Justify the text at the left margin only.
- Double-space text, including:
  - Title page,
  - Notes, and
  - Works Cited.
- Indent the first line of each new paragraph 0.5 inches.
- Only one space after period should be left (unless otherwise advised by your instructor).
- Do not use automatic hyphenation feature for your text.

Printing:
- Use standard white paper, A4 format, 8.5 inches x 11 inches.
- Consult with your instructor to print on a single side or both sides of paper.

3.2 Running Head

Running head is the text line that appears at the right top of every page:

- 0.5 inches from the top and flush right.
- The running head consists of your **surname, a space**, and **a page number**.
- All pages are numbered consecutively throughout the paper starting from the first page:

Example (for a single author):

Turner 5

- If there are several authors, include all authors' surnames:

Example (for several authors):

Turner, Brown, Rodriguez 5

- If all authors' surnames would not fit one line of text, only include the page number:

Example (for too many authors):

5

3.3 First Page (Title Page)

According to MLA guidelines, **a separate title page is not required, normally**:
- Consult with your instructor if a separate title page is requested for your research paper.
- If there are several authors, create a separate title page and list all authors' names there.

On the first page, **in the upper left corner** list:
- **Your full name,**
- **Your instructor's surname** (include all instructors' names),
- **The course name and number,**
- **The date** (day-month-year format).

On a new line, **center the title** of your paper:
- Do not italicize, or place it in quotation marks.
- Use title case capitalization (only first letter of each major word is capitalized).
- Italicize only the parts of title that you would italicize in your text (check Chapter 5.4 for details):
  - *For example:* Analysis of Characters in *The Legend of Sleepy Hollow*
  - *For example:* Difference between *Excuse Me* and *Sorry*
- Do not put a period at the end of your title.

On a new line, **begin the first paragraph** of your text:
- Indent the first line of each new paragraph 0.5 inches:

Example:

White 1

Andrew J. White

Professor Richardson

English 2210

20 April 2021

Literacy Essentials

Lorem ipsum dolor sit amet, consectetur adipiscing elit. Phasellus lorem nulla, fermentum a aliquam sed. Donec aliquet tempor nisi nec sagittis. Duis sed dolor non justo auctor bibendum. Morbi hendrerit nulla ante, et gravida elit aliquet vestibulum. Praesent tincidunt augue massa, ut maximus eros tincidunt sit amet. Nullam consequat venenatis ligula, vitae blandit tellus. Nullam dapibus quam nec tellus lacinia viverra. Mauris lacus magna, pulvinar vitae sagittis non, maximus ac odio. In vestibulum nisl non libero commodo, quis ultricies ex venenatis…

3.4 Headings

Headings in the text organize and structure your paper, but you should avoid overusing them.

Keep the heading short and follow the guidelines:
- Maintain the styling of headings consistent:
  o Each level 1 heading should appear in the same style and size.
  o Each level 2 heading should appear in the same style and size, and so on.
- Style the headings in descending order of prominence:
  o To signal prominence, use different styling and size for the headings:

    ▪ **Larger bold fonts** indicate prominence.
    ▪ *Smaller italicized fonts* indicate subordination.

- Avoid using all capital letters for your headings.
- Avoid using numbers and letters for headings (unless otherwise is advised by your instructor).

- If you decide to have a subheading (level 2 heading), you should have another subheading (level 2 heading) at least, and so on.
- Headings should always be:
  o Flush left,
  o Double-spaced,
  o Not indented,
  o Not centered,
- Use title case capitalization (only first letters of major words should be capitalized).
- Do not put a period at the end of any heading.

The following headings are samples that you can use for your paper. However, you may come up with your system of formatting if needed as long as it does not contradict the above-mentioned guidelines:

Level 1

Heading Level 1: Bold, Flush Left, 13 pt.

Text starts with a new paragraph.

Level 2

Heading Level 2: Plain, Flush Left, 13 pt.

Text starts with a new paragraph.

Level 3

Heading Level 3: Italicized, Flush Left, 12 pt.

Text starts with a new paragraph.

Level 4

Heading Level 4: Plain, Flush Left, 11 pt.

Text starts with a new paragraph.

Level 5

Heading Level 5: Italicized, Flush Left, 11 pt.

Text starts with a new paragraph.

Global Warming (Level 1)

...

Environment (Level 2)

...

Wildlife (Level 2)

...

Flora (Level 3)

...

Fauna (Level 3)

...

Air Pollution (Level 1)

...

Atmosphere (Level 2)

...

Pollution Source (Level 3)

...

Human-Made (Level 4)

...

Cars (Level 5)

...

Factories (Level 5)

...

Natural (Level 4)

...

Animals (Level 5)

...

Sea Salt (Level 5)

...

Fossil Fuels (Level 3)

...

Oil (Level 4)

...

Coal (Level 4)

...

Natural Gas (Level 4)

...

Gasoline (Level 4)

...

Factors (Level 2)

...

3.5 Text Styling

Quotation Marks in Text

- Quotation marks are mainly used for:
  1. Direct quotations,
  2. Styling titles of some works.

- Other minor cases when the quotation marks are used are:
  1. To **mark translations** of words or phrases:
     - Use double or single quotation marks to indicate translation of foreign text.
  2. To **flag provisional meaning**:
     - To indicate skepticism or disapproval:
       - Quotation marks are not used after "so-called":

Example:

The only French phrase I remember is *le ciel est bleu* ("the sky is blue").

The only French phrase I remember is *le ciel est bleu* 'the sky is blue'.

Some "experts" suggest never discussing problems in marriage.

Some so-called experts suggest never discussing problems in marriage.

Italics in Text

Italics are used in text:
1. To indicate when letters and words **are referred to as letters and words** and
2. To **differentiate words** in foreign languages.

Example:

Please, pronounce *known* without the first *k*.

It connects the development of *holla* and its French origin *holà*

3.6 Works Cited

The Works Cited list appears at the very end of your paper:
- Center Works Cited at the top of the new page:
  - If there is only one reference in the list, name it Work Cited instead.
- Each new entry starts with a new line and is flushed left:
  - Subsequent lines of each new entry should be indented 0.5 inches ("hanging indent").
  - Double-spaced.
  - Alphabetized:

Example:

Surname 8

Works Cited

Brown, Sebastian. *Effective Ways of Reducing Air Pollution.* 2014. U of Toronto, PhD dissertation. *ProQuest,* search.proquest.com/docview/0783574542.

Clark, Dominic F. *A Visit to a Village.* Translated by Andrew Parker, Bonnier Books, 2009.

Commonwealth of Nations. *Drug Addiction.* Editis, 2004.

Henderson, Jaxon. "Corruption." *Global Terrorism,* Kodansha, 2014, pp. 334–49.

Live Art: The Awakened Performer. 24 Feb.–5 Mar. 2017, Museum of Fine Arts, Boston.

Nelson, Benjamin. Personal communication with author. 15 May 2021.

Ramirez, Madelyn. "School Uniforms." *Nature Communications,* vol. 45, no. 2, summer 2021, pp. 29–34. *AEBEL,* http://doi.org/1004.3548.5680/chkg77.

Stevenson, Amanda, et al. "The Impact of Contraceptive Access on High School Graduation." *Science Advances,* vol. 7, no. 19, 5 May 2021, https://advances.sciencemag.org/content/7/19/eabf6732.

Ward, Mila. Telephone interview with the author. 22 July 2020.

3.7 Tables, Figures, and Examples

Tables

Tables are any graphics that use rows and columns to structure the content:
- All tables should be numbered with Arabic numerals sequentially.
- Label "Table" is flush left and bold.
- The title of the table should be written in title case on a new line, flush left:
  - Do not put a period at the end of the title.
- For the table body, spacing and alignment are usually enough to determine the cells:
  - Avoid using many horizontal lines,
  - Do not use any vertical lines.
- Indicate the source of the table and place any notes to the table after the table body:
  - Use lowercase letters ([a], [b], [c]) rather than numerals for the notes to the table.
- Double-space throughout:

Example:

Lorem ipsum dolor sit amet, consectetur adipiscing elit. Phasellus lorem nulla, fermentum a aliquam sed. Donec aliquet tempor nisi nec sagittis. Duis sed dolor non justo auctor bibendum. Morbi hendrerit nulla ante, et gravida elit aliquet vestibulum. Praesent tincidunt augue massa, ut maximus eros tincidunt sit amet.

Table 1

Number and Percentage of Students Enrolled in Degree-Granting Postsecondary Institutions[a]

Institution	Number of Students	Percent of Students
Public	14,539,257	65.9
Private	5,112,155	61.3
Nonprofit	4,131,846	69.6
For-profit	980,309	26.6

Adapted from: U.S. Department of Education. *Digest of Education Statistics,* 2020, table 311.15, nces.ed.gov/programs/digest/d20/tables/dt20_311.15.asp.

a. These figures include data for fall 2018 of the 50 states and the District of Columbia and exclude data for fall 2019 and for undergraduate and postbaccalaureate institutions.

Nullam consequat venenatis ligula, vitae blandit tellus. Nullam dapibus quam nec tellus lacinia viverra. Mauris lacus magna, pulvinar vitae sagittis non, maximus ac odio. In vestibulum nisl non libero commodo, quis ultricies ex venenatis.

Figures

Figures are any visuals other than tables and examples:
- o Photograph,
- o Painting,
- o Drawing,
- o Map,
- o Diagram, or
- o Chart.

- All figures should be numbered with Arabic numerals sequentially.
- A label, number, and title usually appear below the illustration, centered and written in one paragraph:
  - o Label "Figure" is usually abbreviated "Fig."
  - o Punctuate the title as a Works Cited list entry.
  - o Do not invert the name of the author.
- If the title of figure provides complete information regarding the source, there is no need to include the source into the Works Cited list:

Example:

Lorem ipsum dolor sit amet, consectetur adipiscing elit. Phasellus lorem nulla, fermentum a aliquam sed.

Donec aliquet tempor nisi nec sagittis. Duis sed dolor non justo auctor bibendum. Morbi hendrerit nulla ante, et

gravida elit aliquet vestibulum. Praesent tincidunt augue massa, ut maximus eros tincidunt sit amet.

Fig. 1. Lawren Harris. *Mountain Forms*. 1926, Museum London.

Nullam consequat venenatis ligula, vitae blandit tellus. Nullam dapibus quam nec tellus lacinia viverra.

Mauris lacus magna, pulvinar vitae sagittis non, maximus ac odio. In vestibulum nisl non libero commodo, quis

ultricies ex venenatis.

Examples

Examples are musical illustrations:
- All examples should be numbered with Arabic numerals sequentially.
- A label, number, and title usually appear below the example, centered and written in one paragraph:
  - Label "Example" is usually abbreviated "Ex."
  - Punctuate the title as a Works Cited list entry.
  - Do not invert the name of the author.
- If the title of example provides complete information regarding the source, there is no need to include the source into the Works Cited list:

Example:

Lorem ipsum dolor sit amet, consectetur adipiscing elit. Phasellus lorem nulla, fermentum a aliquam sed.

Donec aliquet tempor nisi nec sagittis. Duis sed dolor non justo auctor bibendum. Morbi hendrerit nulla ante, et

gravida elit aliquet vestibulum. Praesent tincidunt augue massa, ut maximus eros tincidunt sit amet.

Ex. 1. Abel Korzeniowski, Evgeni's Waltz.

Nullam consequat venenatis ligula, vitae blandit tellus. Nullam dapibus quam nec tellus lacinia viverra.

Mauris lacus magna, pulvinar vitae sagittis non, maximus ac odio. In vestibulum nisl non libero commodo, quis

ultricies ex venenatis.

3.8 Lists

- Lists can be:
    1. Integrated into the sentence, or
    2. Set vertically.
- Lists can also be numbered if enumeration is essential.

Integrated into Sentence

According to MLA guidelines, it is preferable to integrate lists into the text if the items are short:
- To introduce an integrated list, use a colon or an introductory phrase.
- Punctuate items in a list as you would punctuate words in a sentence:

Example:

Accessibility and convenience: the broad variety of products and services, online comparison, adequate buildings, basic and urban infrastructure services, proffered location, public amenities, centralized and smart home system, comfort and security.

OR

Example:

Accessibility and convenience include the broad variety of products and services, online comparison, adequate buildings, basic and urban infrastructure services, proffered location, public amenities, centralized and smart home system, comfort and security.

- If you like to enumerate items in the text, use numerals enclosed in parentheses before each item:

Example:

Accessibility and convenience: (1) the broad variety of products and services, (2) online comparison, (3) adequate buildings, (4) basic and urban infrastructure services, (5) proffered location, (6) public amenities, (7) centralized and smart home system, (8) comfort and security.

Set Vertically

Vertical lists are preferable for lengthy items:
- To introduce a vertical list, use an introductory phrase followed by a colon.
- The items should be consistent throughout the list and can be:
  - Complete sentences or
  - Fragments.
- Use a block indent, 0.5 inches from the left margin for the list:
  - Each item in the list should have an additional hanging indent for all subsequent lines.

Vertical lists can be:
- Unnumbered,
- Numbered, or
- Bulleted.

Unnumbered List with Complete Sentences

- Capitalize the first letter of each item:
  - Follow each item with a closing punctuation (period, question mark, etc.):

Example:

Conversation questions for dreams, daydreams and nightmares offered for students of the ESL classroom:

Do you dream regularly?

What is a daydream?

What is your worst nightmare?

What is the difference between our daydreams and our dreams at night?

What is the difference between our everyday life and dreaming while we are sleeping?

Unnumbered List and Numbered List with Fragments

- Lowercase the first letter of each item.
- Punctuate the fragments as parts of a sentence:
  - Follow each item with semicolons.
  - Write "**and**" or "**or**" before the final item.
  - Follow final item with a period:

Accessibility and convenience:

1. the broad variety of products and services;

2. online comparison;

3. adequate buildings;

4. basic and urban infrastructure services;

5. proffered location;

6. public amenities;

7. centralized and smart home system; and

8. comfort and security.

Bulleted List

- For fragment items, lowercase the first letter of each item:
  - No punctuation follows list item.
- For full-sentence items, capitalize the first letter of each item.
  - Follow each item with a closing punctuation (period, question mark, etc.):

Example (fragment items list):

Accessibility and convenience:

- the broad variety of products and services

- online comparison

- adequate buildings

- basic and urban infrastructure services

- proffered location

- public amenities

- centralized and smart home system

- comfort and security

3.9 Numbers

Number Ranges

For **numbers up to 99**, write the second number in full for a range:
- 1–4
- 23–45

For **larger numbers**, write only the last 2 digits of the second number (unless more numbers are needed for clarity):
- 117–19
- 499–503
- 1,005–08

For **Roman numerals**, write ranges in full:
- i–ii
- ix–xiii

For **alphanumeric numbers**, write ranges in full:
- B21–B23

For **ongoing incomplete ranges**, add a space after the hyphen:
- 2019–

Dates

- Do not abbreviate dates in the text.
- Keep the dates format consistent:
  - The "Day Month Year" format:
    - *For example:* 22 April 2021
  - The "Month Day, Year" format:
    - Put a comma before the year.
    - *For example:* April 22, 2021
- Lowercase season names in dates:
  - winter 2021.
- For decades, spell out or use numerals consistently:
  - The twenties,
  - The 1920s.
- For centuries, spell out the number in lowercase letters:
  - The eighteenth century.
- Write abbreviations BC, BCE, and CE after the year:
  - 12 BC.
- Write abbreviations AD and AH before the year.
  - AH 901.

Time

Use numerals **for most times of the day**:
- Use the 12-hour system:
  - 1:00 a.m.
  - 3:00 p.m.
- To specify the time zone, use an abbreviation or write it in full:
  - 5:00 EST,
  - 10:20 Pacific Standard Time.

Spell out numbers in words **for time followed by o'clock** and expressed in **quarters and half hours**:
- Half past five,
- Seven o'clock.

3.10 Notes (Footnotes and Endnotes)

A note is a supplementary tool to provide commentary or additional information to support the body paragraphs.

There are 2 types of notes:
1. Content notes.
2. Bibliographic notes.

General Format

- Notes may be formatted:
  1. As footnotes:
     - A notes section appearing at the end of the page is separated from the main text with a line.
  2. As endnotes:
     - A notes section appearing at the end of the paper (before the Works Cited) should be titled Notes or Endnotes.
- Consult with your instructor to specify which format is preferred.
- Use **superscript Arabic numerals** ([1], [2], [3]) in the text and notes section to mark notes:
  - Do not put a period after the numeral.
- Double-space all notes.

- **In the text section**, place superscript numerals at the end of sentences (if possible):
  - Place superscript numerals after a punctuation mark:
  - Place superscript numerals before the dash.
- **In the notes section**, use parentheses for page numbers of the source:
  - Omit parentheses if the note only points the reader to the location in source without any additional information:

Example (in the text section):

Liu summarises the main assumption underlying CPTED[1] — namely, that a modification of the physical environment can lead to a reduction in the crime rate. The work focuses on applying approved and tested CPTED strategies to the renewal of urban habitats.[2] The physical causes "lead to increased crime and fear of crime."[3]

Example (in the notes section):

[1] Liu uses their own theory based on the crime rate relation (235).

[2] See Liu 235.

[2] See Liu 236.

Content Notes

Content notes provide detailed commentary that could distract the reader from the main text and allow the writer:

- To explain word choice:
  - To indicate offensive terms that were directly quoted from the source.
- To comment on allusions.
- To provide more examples.
- To specify the scope of research.
- To point to the future research.
- To acknowledge important person.
- To identify authors whose names are written as "et al." etc.:

Example:

[1] Jackson's model is based on theoretical knowledge.

[2] Further investigation is needed for this case.

[3] Andy Howard, the head of our English department, suggested familiarizing myself with

Marcel Schwob.

Bibliographic Notes

Bibliographic notes provide additional information in regards to sources and allow the writer:

- To cite a lengthy thread of sources,
- To mark editions and translations, etc.:

Example:

[1] See Young et al., "How Has the Institution of Marriage Changed in the Postmodern World"

1055; Martin, "The Departed" 996; Butler and Kelly, ch. 8; Thomas, World Torn 111 and "The

Significance of Ethics" 233.

[2] All translations are mine throughout the paper.

3.11 Abbreviations

- Remember that clarity is always more important than economy of space:
  - Spell out the term with words if abbreviation may sound confusing.

Most Common Academic Abbreviations

The following abbreviations are used for the Works Cited list entries and in-text citations:
- To form the plural form of abbreviation, add an "s" without an apostrophe (unless there is a specific form indicated):

Abbreviation	—	Description
app.	—	appendix
ch.	—	chapter
col.	—	column
dept.	—	department
ed.	—	edition
e.g.	—	for example
et al.	—	and others
etc.	—	and so forth
fig.	—	figure
i.e.	—	that is
MS	—	manuscript
MSS	—	manuscripts
n	—	note
nn	—	notes
no.	—	number
nos.	—	numbers
p.	—	page
pp.	—	pages
par.	—	paragraph
qtd.	—	quoted
rev.	—	revised
sec.	—	section
trans.	—	translated by
U	—	University
UP	—	University Press
vers.	—	version
v.	—	versus
vol.	—	volume

4.0 IN-TEXT CITATIONS

4.1 Introduction

In-text citations are short references that link to the Works Cited list for the sources you used in your paper.

MLA format uses the **author-page method** for in-text citations:
- Author's last name and the page number of the source should always be included in the in-text citation.
  - The author's last name can appear in the sentence or in parentheses after the citation.
  - The page number always appears in the parentheses after the citation.

Any in-text citation should correspond to the source listed in the Works Cited and vice versa.

In the text, citations can appear:
1. In prose, or
2. In parentheses.

Citation in Prose	Parenthetical Citation
Daniel Nwaigwe stated that China is the second-largest trading partner of the United States after the EU.	China is the second-largest trading partner of the United States after the EU (Nwaigwe).
According to the article "Modern World," globalization can be explained as "an intensification of social relations worldwide through the linkage of distant localities."	Globalization can be explained as "an intensification of social relations worldwide through the linkage of distant localities" ("Modern World").

4.2 Formatting In-Text Citations

General Format	Author's Surname … (Page Number)	… (Author's Surname Page Number)
Example	Lewis … (68).	… (Lewis 68).
Example in the text	Lewis defined globalization as "the spread of free-market capitalism to all parts of the world" (68).	Globalization is defined as "the spread of free-market capitalism to all parts of the world" (Lewis 68).

Punctuation

- For a standard citation, **no punctuation** is used between the author's name and the page number:

Example:
… (Johnson 28).

- If citation **additionally includes title**, add a comma between the author's name and the title:

Example:
… (Collins, *Healing* 119).

- For a citation of **different pages in a single source,** add commas between different pages:

Example:
… (Turner 335, 476, 543–59).

- For a citation of **multiple sources in a single parenthesis**, add semicolons between different sources:

Example:
… (Gonzalez 71; Thomas 223).

- For a citation of **multiple works by the same author**:
    - For 2 titles, add "and" to join the titles.
    - For 3+ titles, use a comma and "and":

Example:
… (Watson, "Environmental Philosophy" and "Family").   … (Watson, "Environmental Philosophy," "Family," and Preface).

- For a citation **with a personal explanation,** add a semicolon:

Example:
… (Bryant 556; my translation).

Pagination

- For in-text citation, **do not precede** a page number with "**p.**" or "**pp.**"
- **For pages**, always use the same style of numerals as in the original source:
  - Arabic (1, 2, 3)
  - Roman (i, ii, iii)
  - A specialized style:
    - Alphanumeric (A2, B3, B4).

Example:

… (Sanders 123).
… (Henderson xxii–xxv).
… (Campbell 78d).

- For a long quotation that takes several pages in the original source, include **the page range**:

Example:

… (Phillips 6–13).

- If needed, you can add **another location component** instead of a page number:
  - Precede it with an appropriate label to prevent confusion:
    - Chapter,
    - Section,
    - Scene,
    - Paragraph,
    - Line.
  - Always use Arabic numerals even if the numerals in the original source appear otherwise:

Citation in Prose	Parenthetical Citation
chapter 3	… (ch. 3).
section 45	… (sec. 45).
scene 6	… (sc. 6).
paragraph 3	… (par. 3).
line 78	… (line 78).

- For the sources with no page numbers or other numbered sections, add **no number** to your citation:
  - Do not count unnumbered lines, sentences, paragraphs, etc.:

Example:

"The anticipated benefits relate to the purchaser's judgment concerning product quality and ability of the commodity or service to perform certain tasks" (Wright), but she did not offer an explanation as to why.

Commonly Studied Literature

- For **commonly studied prose works and prose plays** provide any other important location additionally to the page number:
  - Use a semicolon to separate the page number and any other information:

Example:

… (Williams 552; ch. 7, sec. 4).

- **Commonly studied poems and verse plays** may contain line numbers in the margins:
  - In this case, omit page numbers and cite by:
    - Section:
      - Act,
      - Scene,
      - Part, etc.
    - Line.
  - Use periods to separate the numbers.
- Act 2, scene 3, lines 46–68 of Shakespeare's play "Romeo and Juliet" would be cited as:

Example:

… (Romeo and Juliet 2.3.46–68).

- To cite note from the source, follow the page number in your citation by appropriate abbreviations:
  - **n** for the note number,
  - **nn** for the notes numbers,
  - **un** for unnumbered note.
- Pay attention to the spaces in the example:

Example:
... (Walker 23n6). ... (Walker 23nn6–9). ... (Walker 23 nn 6, 8, 9). ... (Edwards 46 un).

Time Stamps

- For **audio and video recordings**, add the relevant time or time range:
  - Provide the numbers of hours, minutes, and seconds in the same order (hh:mm:ss),
  - Use colons with no space to separate the numbers of hours, minutes, and seconds:

Example:
... ("*Science*" 00:05:35–49).

4.3 Titles of Sources

Shortening Titles

- When a title is included in a parenthetical citation, shorten it if the title is longer than **a noun phrase**:
  - Shorten the title to the first noun with any preceding adjectives,
  - Exclude any initial article "A", "An", "The":

Full Titles Example	Shortened Titles Example
The Live Art: Awakened Performer	Live Art
"Studies of the Piece Explained: Nonviolence in Action"	"Studies"
"We Create Movement in an Early Childhood Montessori Classroom"	"We"

- If the title **does not begin with a noun phrase**, stop at the end of the first phrase or at the first punctuation mark:

Full Titles Example	Shortened Titles Example
How to Positively Affect Early Childhood Development	How to Positively Affect
In the Time of Forensic Medicine and Anatomy Research	In the Time
Among Short, Long and Wide	Among Short

- If you shorten the title that **contains internal single quotation marks**, leave the single quotation marks within double quotation marks:

Full Titles Example	Shortened Titles Example
"'The Boar Year' and Jackie Robinson"	"'The Boar Year'"

- If the title is short itself or it presents **a rhetorical question**, leave the full title:

Example:
"Am I Chosen One?"

4.4 Authors

1 Author

- Provide the author's last name and a page number:
  - o If you provide the author's last name within the signal phrase in prose, do not add it in the parenthetical citation:

Citation in Prose	Parenthetical Citation
Lewis defined globalization as "the spread of free-market capitalism to all parts of the world" (68).	Globalization is defined as "the spread of free-market capitalism to all parts of the world" (Lewis 68).

2 Authors

- Provide both authors' names and a page number:
  - o If you name the authors for the first time in prose, include both first names and last names.
  - o Provide only surnames with "and" in the parenthetical citation:

Citation in Prose	Parenthetical Citation
Adam Reed and Victor Hernandez note, other than making sure the economic interactions in the region are active and peaceful the Silk Road will also act as an economic and infrastructure incentive (8).	Other than making sure the economic interactions in the region are active and peaceful the Silk Road will also act as an economic and infrastructure incentive (Reed and Hernandez 8).

3+ Authors

- Provide the first author's name followed by "et al." and a page number in the parenthetical citation:
  - o In prose you may name all authors, or provide the first author's name followed by "and others" or "and colleagues":

Citation in Prose	Parenthetical Citation
Ross Campbell and colleagues also revealed weak possibility (21).	The authors also revealed weak possibility (Campbell et al. 21).

Organization as Author

- For a corporate author (an organization), shorten the name to the noun phrase with any preceding adjectives:
    - Exclude any initial article "A", "An", "The":

Citation in Prose	Parenthetical Citation
According to a study by The Psychospiritual Institution of Nature in Healing, it affects people of any age, race, gender, and sex (223).	As one of the studies shows, it affects people of any age, race, gender, and sex (Psychospiritual Institution 223).

2+ Authors with the Same Name

- Add the author's first initial to the author's last name and a page number to prevent confusion with another author with the same last name:
    - If the authors' names begin with the same initials, provide full names in parenthetical citations instead of initials.
    - In prose, always provide the author's first name additionally to the last name to prevent confusion with another author:

Citation in Prose	Parenthetical Citation
As Kim Butler highlights, it is mostly caused by persistent insults, harsh criticism, name-calling, mocking, and humiliations (921).	It is mostly caused by persistent insults, harsh criticism, name-calling, mocking, and humiliations (K. Butler 921).

2+ Works by the Same Author

- Provide a particular title of work to your citation to prevent confusion with another work by the same author:
  - There are several ways to cite such sources:

Author's name and title in prose	Author's name in prose and title in parenthetical citation	Author's name and title in parenthetical citation
As Griffin shows in *Domestic Violence,* many people who find themselves in domestic violence sometimes try to justify the abuser's actions, "they protect them, blame themselves, or even justify their actions thinking that things would get better" (97).	As Griffin shows, many people who find themselves in domestic violence sometimes try to justify the abuser's actions, "they protect them, blame themselves, or even justify their actions thinking that things would get better" (*Domestic Violence* 97).	Many people who find themselves in domestic violence sometimes try to justify the abuser's actions, "they protect them, blame themselves, or even justify their actions thinking that things would get better" (Griffin, *Domestic Violence* 97).

2+ Sources for the Same Citation

- Use semicolons to separate multiple sources in a single parenthesis:
  - Choose the order you like most:
    - Alphabetically,
    - By date,
    - By importance:

Example:
… (Clark 26; Foster 445).

Same Author and Same Title

If several works by the same author have the same title:
- Provide unique piece of information from each entry for in-text citation in square brackets after the title:
  - The edition number,
  - The contributor name:
    - Editor,
    - Translator,
  - Publisher,
  - Publication date:

Example:
… (Simmons [2nd ed.] 94). … (Alexander, *Nature* [HarperCollins] 27).

No Author

- For the work with no author, use the shortened title both in prose and in parentheses instead of the author's name:
  - Use italics or quotation marks depending on the entry in the Works Cited list:

Citation in Prose	Parenthetical Citation
Peace Study notes that after the civil war, there was a need for establishing America's presence overseas, and as such, it was necessary to build bases in other regions (14).	After the civil war, there was a need for establishing America's presence overseas, and as such, it was necessary to build bases in other regions (*Peace Study* 14).

Multivolume Works

- Provide volume number and page number in the parenthetical citation:
    - Use a colon and a space to separate volume and page.
    - Do not use the identifiers **"volume" and "page"**:

Example:

Young writes, "It was necessary for America to build more ships for their merchants to prevent merchants from their biggest competitors from controlling their territories" (2: 45). However, opponents of imperialism argue that "it goes against America's principles of freedom since imperialism entailed conquering and submission of people against their will" (4: xvi).

Scripture

- The names of scripture (Bible, Genesis, Koran, etc.) **are not italicized in prose.**
- The names of scripture written **in full and shortened titles of specific editions are italicized**:
    - If all citations refer to the same edition of the scripture, list only the book, chapter, and verse in the parenthetical citation:

Example:

The Bible ... (*New Jerusalem Bible*, Ezek. 1.2).

Indirect Source

- Generally, indirect sources (sources cited in other sources) should be avoided:
    - Use the abbreviation "qtd. in" (for quoted in) before the indirect source in the parenthetical citation:

Example:

Clark admitted that "Green's bad behaviors could occur at any stage of life relative to the influence of other psychologic factors" (qtd. in Williams 289).

4.5 Quotations and Paraphrases

Always cite the sources you consulted, whether you paraphrase or quote, except for:
- Common knowledge:
  - ○ Information widely available,
  - ○ Basic biographical facts about famous people,
  - ○ Historical events, etc.
- Allusions for rhetorical effect:
  - ○ *For example:* The main character's "to be or not to be" situation had occurred by the moment he received an invitation.
- Passing mentions:
  - ○ Sharing an opinion about the favorite movie is a passing mention.
- Epigraphs:
  - ○ Epigraphs are short quotations at the beginning of the work that establish a special mood.
  - ○ Epigraphs are not included in the Works Cited.

There are **2 methods to properly give credits** to the sources you refer to in your paper:
1. Paraphrasing,
2. Quoting.

Paraphrases

Paraphrasing is referring to a general idea of another work **in your own words**:
- Always provide an in-text citation directing to the Works Cited list:
  - ○ Include the author's name,
  - ○ Include the location of the source (page number, etc.) where the idea is taken from:

Example:
As Rodriguez argues, it was a reflection that the nature of people was in a position to push development in the country a notch higher (64).

Quotations

Quoting is **an exact reproduction** of original words, phrases, sentences, or passages from the source:
- Use double quotation marks to indicate the borrowed part from the source.
- Always provide an in-text citation directing to the Works Cited list:
  - ○ Include the author's name,
  - ○ Include the location of the source (page number, etc.) where the idea is taken from:
- Citations are placed at the end of quotation.
- While quoting, avoid making any changes in:
  - ○ Capitalization,
  - ○ Italicization,
  - ○ Spelling,
  - ○ Punctuation,
  - ○ Accents.
- While quoting, reproduce spelling exactly as in the source:
  - ○ à, ä, é, ê, ç, etc.

There are 2 types of quotations:
1. **Short quotations:**
   - Take less than 4 lines in the text.
2. **Long quotations:**
   - Take more than 4 lines in the text.

If the quotation takes **no more than 4 lines** of text in your paper, incorporate it into your text within double quotation marks:

- If the sentence ends with a quotation, place the parenthetical citation **between the closing quotation mark and the period**:

Example:

Meryl Adams highlights, "The normal functioning of organs like the liver and kidney are adversely affected by alcohol consumption in excess" (19).

- Instead of complete sentences, you may quote **one word or phrase**:
  - Lowercase the first word in a quotation:

Example:

Daniel Howard considers them "intrigued" to a particular individual for a minute (88).

- For a short (2–3 replicas) **dialogue quotation**, integrate it into your prose as in the example:

Example:

When Emily asks "Am I right?," John replies quickly, "Yes, you are. I'm sorry!" (1.3.309–10)

- For a short (2–3 lines) **poetry quotation**, integrate it into your prose as in the example:
  - To mark a break at the end of each line, use a slash with space on each side (/),
  - To mark a stanza break, use a double slash with space on each side (//):

Example:

Emily Gallacher writes, "Fifth, become a respected attending in intensive care / Bark orders at residents, rest easy in your big house."

- If the quotation takes **more than 4 lines** of text in your paper, set it off from the text as a block:
  - Indent the entire block 0.5 inches from the left margin.
  - Do not add quotation marks to the block.
  - Do not indent the first line of quotation.
  - Introductory phrase is followed by a colon.
  - Place the parenthetical citation **after the closing punctuation mark** of a quotation:

Example:

In *Science,* Sanchez names main figures:

> In September 2017, a Brexit debate was held at the Society's Annual General Meeting to discuss the process of Brexit and how it might affect the lives of microbiologists. The Society's General Secretary, Professor Maggie Smith, was joined by Professor Graeme Reid, Chair of the Campaign for Science & Engineering, who is a member of the Government's High Level Forum on Science and Brexit. (28)

- For a long **dialogue quotation** from a non-dramatic prose work (novel, etc.), set it off as a block:
  - Do not add quotation marks to the block.
  - Indent the block 0.5 inches.
  - Reproduce the indentation of dialogue as in the original source.
  - Use double quotation marks for replicas:

Example:

In one of the first dialogues in Jane Austen's *Pride and Prejudice*, we can see how husband's attention is drawn:

> "My dear Mr. Bennet," said his lady to him one day, "have you heard that Netherfield Park is let at last?"
>
> Mr. Bennet replied that he had not.
>
> "But it is," returned she; "for Mrs. Long has just been here, and she told me all about it."
>
> Mr. Bennet made no answer. (55)

- For a long (3+ lines) **poetry quotation**, set it off as a block:
  - Do not add quotation marks.
  - Indent the block 0.5 inches.
  - Place the citation after the quotation on the same line:
    - If the citation does not fit on the same line, place it on a new line, flush right:

> Even so my sun one early morn did shine
>
> With all-triumphant splendour on my brow;
>
> But out, alack! he was but one hour mine;
>
> The region cloud hath mask'd him from me now.
>
> Yet him for this my love no whit disdaineth;
>
> Suns of the world may stain when heaven's sun staineth.
>
> (Shakespeare, sonnet 33)

- For **a play or screenplay quotation**, set it off as a block:
  - Do not add quotation marks.
  - Indent the block 0.5 inches.
  - Identify each speaker by the appropriate label:
    - Write the label in all capital letters.
    - Follow the label with a period.
  - Provide an additional hanging indent for all subsequent lines of each replica:

Larson's play *Blondes Prefer Gentlemen* contains multiple serious dramatic scenes:

> HE. Thank you. Thank you so much. I don't know how to repay you for this. I think she was going
>
> to kill me.
>
> SHE. That's the easy way out. I think you should have to live and suffer for what you've done.
>
> HE. I'll give you anything. Please just let me go. (345–47)

Making Changes to Quotations

Omitting the Part of Quotation

- Whenever you omit words, phrases, or sentences, make sure it would not confuse or cause misunderstanding for your reader:
  - Use **an ellipsis** with a space before and after or **three spaced periods** (. . .) to indicate that some part of the quote has been left out:

Example:
According to Adam Reed and Victor Hernandez, "Other than making sure the economic interactions in the region are active and peaceful . . . the Silk Road will also act as an economic and infrastructure incentive" (8).

- To mark lines omission in the poetry quotation, use **a line of spaced periods** (. . . . .) approximately the length of an average line:

Example:

Alfred Tennyson's "Tears, Idle Tears" is a great example:
 	
    Ah, sad and strange as in dark summer dawns
 	
    . . . .
 	
    The casement slowly grows a glimmering square;
 	
    So sad, so strange, the days that are no more.

Adding to or Clarifying the Quotation

- If you need to add an explanation to the quotation, use **square brackets** ([]):
  - To prevent context misunderstanding,
  - To explain the meaning of a particular part:

Example:
In the view of Brooks, "the [Senate election] results are in sync with states' presidential votes."

Adding Emphasis

- For rare cases when emphasis is needed, **italicize words** you like to emphasize:
  - After the quotation, add "emphasis added" in parentheses:

Example:

According to Brooks, "the results reflected *local* patterns" (emphasis added).

Fixing Errors

- To mark a spelling or grammatical error made in an original source, add **[sic]** (from Latin "thus" or "so") immediately after the error in the quotation:

Example:

In the view of Jenkins, "Impaired judgment, nausea, laziness and impractical crave for food leads [sic] to general body malfunctions" (71).

Changing Syntax

- To fit quotation grammatically into your sentence, you may change the syntax (tense of a verb, etc.):
  - To mark any changes, use **square brackets** ([]):

Example:

If Patterson could comment on it, she would likely say, "It [is] a living thing!"

5.0 WORKS CITED

5.1 General Guidelines

Each source cited in the prose must be included in the list of Works Cited and vice versa:
- Place the list of Works Cited at the very end of your paper (after notes if any).
- Title the list "Works Cited", centered:
  - To additionally include sources that were consulted for the project but not cited in the paper, title the list "Works Cited and Consulted" instead.
- Double-space all entries.
- Indent subsequent lines of each entry by 0.5 inches (a hanging indent).
- For the titles of sources, use title case capitalization (all major words are capitalized):
  - Use italics for titles of larger works that contain other works:
    - Book,
    - Newspaper,
    - Magazine, etc.
  - Use quotation marks for titles of shorter works:
    - Article,
    - Webpage,
    - Poem, etc.
- Alphabetize entries by authors (or titles for the entries with no author):
  - Ignore initial articles "A", "An", "The" when alphabetizing by titles.
- End each entry with a period.

5.2 MLA Template of Core Elements

To create any Works Cited list entry, use the following MLA template of core elements:

1	Author.
2	Title of Source.

Container:

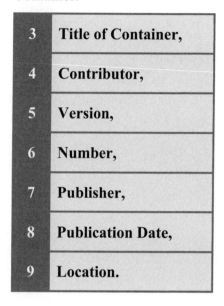

3	Title of Container,
4	Contributor,
5	Version,
6	Number,
7	Publisher,
8	Publication Date,
9	Location.

To create Works Cited list entry for a particular source, choose the relevant elements from the template above:

- Any element from the template can be skipped except for the "Title of Source" element:
  - For a source with no title, provide a brief description of the work in your words.
- List elements in the established order as shown in the template:
  - Follow each element with the punctuation mark as shown in the template.
- End the entry with a period.

1. Author

Use the "Author" element to include the author of work in your Works Cited list entry:

Example:
Hughes, John. "Writing and Performance." *Human Resource and Sustainability Studies,* translated by Brian Cox, 2nd ed., vol. 4, no. 13, Oxford UP, 2021, pp. 104–12.

First author's name should always be **reversed**:
- Begin an entry with the author's last name:
- Follow the author's last name with a comma and the rest of the name as given in the original source.
- End with a period.

2. Title of Source

Use the "Title of Source" element to include the title of work in your Works Cited list entry:

Example:

Hughes, John. "Writing and Performance." *Human Resource and Sustainability Studies,* translated by

Brian Cox, 2nd ed., vol. 4, no. 13, Oxford UP, 2021, pp. 104–12.

- For the titles of sources, use title case capitalization (all major words are capitalized):
  - Use italics for titles of larger works that contain other (shorter) works:
    - Book,
    - Newspaper,
    - Magazine, etc.
  - Use quotation marks for titles of shorter works:
    - Article,
    - Webpage,
    - Poem, etc.
- For a source with no title, **provide a brief description** of the work in your words:
  - Capitalize the first letter of the first word of description and proper nouns.
  - Do not italicize or enclose the description in quotation marks.
  - For punctuation, treat the description as a standard phrase in the text:
- End with a period:

Example:

Walker, Lucas. Photo of Olivia Brown's house for selling. *Facebook*, 19 May 2021,

  www.facebook.com/356875478560/.

Advertisement for real estate in Canada. *Editis*, 2021, p. 3.

---

3. Title of Container

Use the "Title of Container" element to include the bigger work that contains another work in your Works Cited list entry:

Example:

Hughes, John. "Writing and Performance." *Human Resource and Sustainability Studies,* translated by

Brian Cox, 2nd ed., vol. 4, no. 13, Oxford UP, 2021, pp. 104–12.

For the titles of containers, use title case capitalization (all major words are capitalized):
- Italicize the titles of containers:
  - Periodicals,
  - Anthologies,
  - Websites, etc.:

Container (bigger work that contains another shorter work)	Shorter works
Periodical: o Journal o Newspaper o Magazine	**Article in periodical:** o Article in journal o Article in newspaper o Article in magazine o A review
Anthology	o Short story o Poem o Essay
Website	o Post o Comment o Review o Video o Song
CD Album	o Song
TV Show	o Episode o Podcast

4. Contributor

Use the "Contributor" element to include the contributors of work in your Works Cited list entry:

Example:

Hughes, John. "Writing and Performance." *Human Resource and Sustainability Studies,* translated by

Brian Cox, 2nd ed., vol. 4, no. 13, Oxford UP, 2021, pp. 104–12.

The contributors are secondary creators and they should be acknowledged in the entry:
- Style the names as any other authors' names:
  - Do not reverse the names of contributors.
- For 3+ contributors, list only the first contributor's name followed by "et al."
- Precede the contributor's name with a label of the contributor's role:

Label of Contributor's Role	Contributors
<ul><li>edited by</li><li>translated by</li><li>illustrated by</li><li>narrated by</li><li>directed by</li><li>created by</li><li>uploaded by</li><li>adapted by</li><li>conducted by</li><li>performance by</li></ul>	<ul><li>Editors,</li><li>Translators,</li><li>Illustrators,</li><li>The narrator of an audiobook,</li><li>The director of a film,</li><li>The creator of a TV show,</li><li>The person responsible for uploading a video, etc.</li></ul>

5. Version

Use the "Version" element to include the form or version of work in your Works Cited list entry:

Example:
Hughes, John. "Writing and Performance." *Human Resource and Sustainability Studies,* translated by Brian Cox, 2nd ed., vol. 4, no. 13, Oxford UP, 2021, pp. 104–12.

- Versions mostly refer to:
  - Editions of books and
  - Revised editions of books.
- Use ordinal numbers with Arabic numerals for versions:
  - 3rd
  - 12th
- Follow the number of version with an appropriate abbreviation:

Version	Abbreviation
Edition	ed.
Revised	rev.

6. Number

Use the "Number" element to include the number of a sequenced work in your Works Cited list entry:

> **Example:**
>
> Hughes, John. "Writing and Performance." *Human Resource and Sustainability Studies,* translated by
>
> Brian Cox, 2nd ed., vol. 4, no. 13, Oxford UP, 2021, pp. 104–12.

For the sequenced work, include the number of work in series:
- Preceded the number by a term that identifies the kind of division.
- Use Arabic numerals:
  - Convert Roman numbers and spelled out in words numbers into Arabic numerals:

In the original source	In the Work Cited list
Volume 5, Number 66	vol. 5, no. 66
Volume VII, Num. Three	vol. 7, no. 3
Volume 3, Numbers 12–13	vol. 3, nos. 12–13
S4:E15	season 4, episode 15
Episode 4 of Season One	season 1, episode 4

7. Publisher

Use the "Publisher" element to include the publisher or distributor of work in your Works Cited list entry:

Example:

Hughes, John. "Writing and Performance." *Human Resource and Sustainability Studies,* translated by

Brian Cox, 2nd ed., vol. 4, no. 13, Oxford UP, 2021, pp. 104–12.

Include the primarily responsible publisher of work:
- The publisher of a book.
- The website, company, organization.
- The studio, theater company, network, and other distributors that produced a film, show, play, etc.
- The agency that produced a government publication.

For the sources with several publishers, list all publishers relevant to the paper:
- Use **common academic abbreviations**:

In the Source	In the Entry
Cambridge University Press University of the Philippines Press	Cambridge UP U of the Philippines P

- Replace **an ampersand (&)** or a **plus sign (+)** with **"and"** in a publisher's name:

In the Source	In the Entry
Simon & Schuster John Wiley + Sons	Simon and Schuster John Wiley and Sons

- Separate publishers with **a forward slash (/)**:

In the Source	In the Entry
Hachette Livre and Oxford University Press	Hachette Livre / Oxford UP

8. Publication Date

Use the "Publication Date" element to include the date of publication in your Works Cited list entry:

Example:

Hughes, John. "Writing and Performance." *Human Resource and Sustainability Studies,* translated by

Brian Cox, 2nd ed., vol. 4, no. 13, Oxford UP, 2021, pp. 104–12.

The date of publication can take one of the following forms:
- A year,
- A day, month, and year,
- A season and year,
- A range of dates and years,
- A time stamp.

Use **"Day Month Year"** format:
- Provide the most specific date.

For the sources with **approximate dates**, reproduce the date as given in the source:
- late 16th century,
- circa 1310–20.

Lowercase seasons names:
- summer 2018,
- winter 2021.

Write the month in full if it has **4 letters or less**:
- May
- June
- July

Abbreviate the month if it has **more than 4 letters**:
- Dec.
- Jan.
- Feb.
- Mar.
- Apr.
- Aug.
- Sept.
- Oct.
- Nov.

9. Location

Use the "Location" element to include the location of work in your Works Cited list entry:

Location depends on the format of source:
- For printed works, the location is presented as a page or page range.
- For electronic works, the location is presented as DOI or URL:

Example:

Hughes, John. "Writing and Performance." *Human Resource and Sustainability Studies,* translated by

Brian Cox, 2nd ed., vol. 4, no. 13, Oxford UP, 2021, pp. 104–12.

Cooper, Nina. "Environmental Philosophy." *Cancer Therapy*, vol. 3, no. 14, 2009,

http://doi.org/1024.3455.5552/x0r68.

For **printed works**, include the page or page range:
- Use the appropriate abbreviation:
  - p. for a single page,
  - pp. for a range of pages.
- Always use the same style of numerals as in the original source:
  - Arabic (1, 2, 3)
  - Roman (i, ii, I, II)
  - Alphanumeric (B23, 73c).

For **works that can be accessed online**, include DOI or URL:
- DOI is digital object identifier:
  - Always **include the protocol (http:// or https://) with DOIs.**
- URL is uniform resource locator:
  - Generally, **omit the protocol (http:// or https://) for the URLs.**
- DOI is preferred over a URL.

DOI	*URL*
A DOI (digital object identifier) is an identification number assigned by the publisher that never changes and links reader to the document on the Internet: • DOI is preferred over a URL. • When available include DOIs in the Works Cited list entries instead of URLs. • Always **include the protocol (http:// or https://)** with DOIs in the Works Cited list entries:	URLs (uniform resource locators) consist of: • The protocol (http:// or https://). • The website address (www.website.com). • The path (the rest of the link). Generally, **omit the protocol (http:// or https://) for the URLs** in the Works Cited list entries unless you need to hyperlink them:
https://doi.org/xxxx.xxxx.xxxx	www.amazon.com/Appearance-Publishers/e/B091TLWPW9/

Supplemental (Optional) Elements

- To provide additional information about work, add a "Supplemental" element to the template:

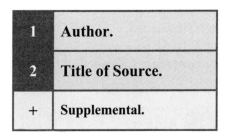

Container:

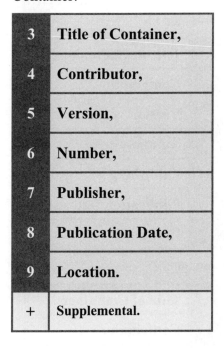

Provide as much additional information as needed to "Supplemental" element:
- Separate items with a comma.
- End supplemental element with a period.

Items, placed after "Title of Source":	Items, placed at the end of entry:

• Contributor
• Original date of publication
	• Date of access
	• Book series
	• Multivolume works
	• Medium of publication:
	   ○ Oil on canvas
	   ○ Marble sculpture
	   ○ Transcript
	   ○ PDF download, etc.
	• Dissertations and theses
	• Government documents
	• Publication history

Complex Works

More complex works are *works that are contained in other works which are also contained in other works*:

- Article from a journal contained in a database,
- Poem from a book contained in series, etc.

For more complex works, add **as many containers as needed** to provide the full Works Cited list entry:

1	**Author.**
2	**Title of Source.**

Container 1:

3	**Title of Container 1,**
4	**Contributor,**
5	**Version,**
6	**Number,**
7	**Publisher,**
8	**Publication Date,**
9	**Location.**

Container 2:

3	**Title of Container 2,**
4	**Contributor,**
5	**Version,**
6	**Number,**
7	**Publisher,**
8	**Publication Date,**
9	**Location.**

5.3 Authors

1 Author

- Begin an entry with the author's last name:
  - Follow the author's last name with a comma and the rest of the name as given in the original source.
  - End with a period:

Example:

Campbell, Asher J. *Religion and Psychology.* Springer Nature, 2016.

Cooper, Nina. "Environmental Philosophy." *Cancer Therapy*, vol. 3, no. 14, 2009,

　　　http://doi.org/1024.3455.5552/x0r68.

2 Authors

- Provide both author' names in the entry:
  - Begin an entry with the first author's name:
    - Reverse it as described above
  - Follow the first author's name with **a comma and "and"** to distinguish two authors' names.
  - Provide the second author's name in the normal order.
  - End with a period:

Example:

Hernandez, Leo, and Natalie Jackson. *Adventure According to Humphrey.* Penguin Random House,

　　　2020.

3+ Authors

- Provide only the first author's name (reversed) followed by "et al." ("and others"):
    - Do not italicize "et al.":

Example:

Oliveira, Paulo, et al. "Impact of Delays on Customers' Safety Perceptions and Behavioral Intentions."

Journal of Airline and Airport Management, vol. 2, no. 2, 2012, pp. 86–100.

Organization as Author

- For a corporate author (an organization), exclude any initial article "A", "An", "The":

Example:

Cardigans. *Life*. Trampolene Records, 1995.

Commonwealth of Nations. *Ecologically and Socially Just Worldview*. McGraw-Hill Education, 2019.

No Author

- Skip the Author element if the source has no author:
    - Begin an entry with the title of work.
    - Do not replace the missing author's name with "Anonymous":

Example:

Minerals and Materials Characterization. National Academy of Sciences, 2016.

Pseudonyms

- To list the work published **under the pseudonym**:
  - Begin an entry with the pseudonym appearing in the source.
  - Provide the author's real name in square brackets:

Example:

Johnson, Charles [Caleb Reed]. *Dogs Escape from Frank Einstein.* Bonnier Books, 2013.

Wilson, J. [Charles Bailey]. *Fish in Water.* Penguin Random House, 1988.

- Alternatively, you may list the work **under the author's real name**:
  - Begin an entry with the author's real name.
  - Provide the pseudonym in square brackets:
    - Precede the pseudonym with "*published as*" in italics:

Example:

Reed, Caleb [*published as* Charles Johnson]. *Dogs Escape from Frank Einstein.* Bonnier Books, 2013.

Bailey, Charles [*published as* J. Wilson]. *Fish in Water.* Penguin Random House, 1988.

Online Author

- If the author's nickname differs from the author's name, you may add the author's nickname in square brackets after the name:

Example:

Mitchell, Ryan [@MitwithRy]. Photo of *Vogue* cover. *Instagram*, 28 Mar. 2021,

    www.instagram.com/p/Bdk_fB6FdkgqPw/.

- For **several works by the same author**, alphabetize the entries by the titles at first:
    - Provide the author's name in the first entry only.
    - For other entries, substitute repeated author's name with three hyphens or three em dashes (———):

Example:

Peer, Marisa. *Diabetes Mellitus.* Macmillan Publishers, 2018.

———. "Immune Based Therapies, Vaccines and Antimicrobials." *Food and Nutrition Sciences*, vol.

6, no. 14, Jan. 2021, p. 44.

- For several works with **the same first author and different coauthors**, order the single-authored work before the co-written works:
    - Do not substitute the first author's name with three em dashes or three hyphens:

Example:

Walker, Jack. *A Boy Called Bat.* Hachette Livre, 2004.

Walker, Jack, and Sofia Simmons. *For the Sake of Our Future.* Pearson Education, 2008.

Walker, Jack, et al. *Interrelationships between Self, Art and Oppression.* Simon & Schuster, 1999.

5.4 Titles of Sources

- In the Works Cited list, write the title of the works in full exactly as they appear in the original source, except:
    1. Capitalization,
    2. Punctuation (for main titles and subtitles),
    3. Styling.
- Generally, follow the Title of Source element with a period:
    o Follow the title with an exclamation point or a question mark if it is a part of the title instead.

1. Capitalization

Reproduce the title exactly as it appears in the original source:
- Do not reproduce "all uppercase" or "all lowercase" letters.
- Use title case capitalization.
- Use a colon between the title and the subtitle:

DO CAPITALIZE	Don't capitalize
<ul><li>Nouns</li><li>Pronouns</li><li>Verbs</li><li>Adjectives</li><li>Adverbs</li><li>Subordinating conjunctions:<ul><li>That</li><li>If</li><li>As If</li><li>As Soon As</li><li>Although</li><li>Because</li><li>Unless</li><li>Till</li><li>Until</li><li>How</li><li>When</li><li>Where</li><li>While</li><li>Who</li><li>Why</li><li>Before</li><li>After</li></ul></li></ul>	<ul><li>Articles:<ul><li>a</li><li>an</li><li>the</li></ul></li><li>Coordinating conjunctions:<ul><li>and</li><li>or</li><li>but</li><li>nor</li><li>yet</li><li>for</li><li>so</li></ul></li><li>Prepositions:<ul><li>between</li><li>against</li><li>according to</li><li>to</li><li>in</li><li>at</li><li>on</li><li>of</li><li>as</li></ul></li><li>The infinitive "to"</li></ul>

2. Punctuation

- For a title with a subtitle, **use a colon before the subtitle** even if the original source does not contain any punctuation between the title and the subtitle:
  - Always capitalize the first letter of the subtitle:

The Live Art: Awakened Performer

- For titles with several subtitles, **use a colon before each subtitle:**
  - Always capitalize the first letter of the subtitle:

MLA Handbook Simplified: Concise Guide to the MLA: Quick Study Guidelines

- For titles with subtitles that are separated with an exclamation point, question mark, or dash in the original source, **do not use a colon**:
  - Use the original source's punctuation instead:

Deep Breathing? A Means for Autistic People to Reconnect with Their Bodies

- For titles that end with a quotation mark, **use a colon after the closing quotation mark** to separate the title and the subtitle:

"Eat, Pray, Love": One Woman's Search for Everything Across Italy, India and Indonesia

- For titles that end with a quotation mark and require a period, **place the period before the closing quotation mark**:

"We Create Movement in an Early Childhood Montessori Classroom."

- For double or alternative titles that begin with "or", **use a semicolon** after the first title **and follow with "or,"** to separate two titles:
  - Always capitalize the first letter of the second title:

Communication Skills; or, Adventure in Building Communication with Children

- For a title with **an ampersand ("&")**, convert it to "and":
  - Use a serial comma:

The Food and Nutrition in Fall, Winter, Spring, and Summer

3. Styling

Generally, the titles in your paper should be:
1. Italicized or
2. Enclosed in double quotation marks.

Italicize the titles of:
- Long independent works.
- Works that contain other works.

Enclose in double quotation marks (""") the titles of:
- Short works,
- Works that are contained in other works.

Titles in Quotation Marks	Italicized Titles	Not Formatted Titles
<ul><li>"Journal Article"</li><li>"Magazine Article"</li><li>"Newspaper Article"</li><li>"Chapter in a Book"</li><li>"Page on a Website"</li><li>"Episode of a TV show"</li><li>"Article"</li><li>"Short Story"</li><li>"Video"</li><li>"Song"</li><li>"Lecture"</li></ul>	<ul><li>*Book*</li><li>*Journal*</li><li>*Magazine*</li><li>*Newspaper*</li><li>*Dissertation*</li><li>*Play*</li><li>*Website*</li><li>*Film*</li><li>*TV Show*</li><li>*Radio Program*</li><li>*Music Album*</li><li>*Visual Art*</li><li>*Court Case*</li></ul>	<ul><li>Scripture:<ul><li>Bible</li><li>Genesis</li><li>Gospels</li><li>Koran</li><li>Old Testament</li><li>Talmud</li></ul></li><li>Musical compositions</li><li>Architectural buildings</li><li>Ancient artworks</li><li>Conferences & Courses</li><li>Laws & Acts</li></ul>

- For the title that contains quotation marks in the original source, use **single quotation marks for the internal title** instead to enclose the entire title in double quotation marks:

"'The Boar Year' and Jackie Robinson"

For a **source with no title**, provide a brief description in your words:
- Capitalize the first letter of the first word of description and proper nouns.
- Do not italicize or enclose the description in quotation marks.
- For punctuation, treat the description as a standard phrase in the text:

Example:

Walker, Lucas. Photo of Olivia Brown's house for selling. *Facebook*, 19 May 2021,

www.facebook.com/356875478560/.

6.0 IN-TEXT CITATIONS / WORKS CITED EXAMPLES

6.1 General Format

Works Cited Entry	In-Text Citation
Author's Last Name, First Name. "Title" (in italics or quotation marks). *Title of Container*, Contributors (translators or editors), Version (edition), Number (vol.# and/or no.#), Publisher, Date, Location (pages, URL, or DOI). 2nd Container's Title, Contributors, Version, Number, Publisher, Date, Location, Date of Access (if applicable).	(Author's Last Name Page)

6.2 Books

General Format:

Author's Last Name, First Name. *Book Title: Book Subtitle*. Publisher, Date.

1 Author

Works Cited Entry	In-Text Citation
Garcia, Savannah. *A Surprise Birthday Party: When the Last Bell Goes.* HarperCollins, 2018.	(Garcia 79)

2 Authors

For the book with 2 authors:
- Start with the first author's name in "last name, first name" format.
- Present following author's name in normal order ("first name last name" format):

Works Cited Entry	In-Text Citation
Jackson, Addison, and Santiago Brooks. *A Journey in an Overcrowded Bus*. Scholastic, 2021.	(Jackson and Brooks 34)

3+ Authors

For the book with 3 or more authors:
- Start with the first author's name in "last name, first name" format followed by "et al.":

Works Cited Entry	In-Text Citation
Coleman, Aurora, et al. *Healthy Lifestyle*. McGraw-Hill Education, 2020.	(Coleman et al. 25)

Organization as Author

- If the author is corporate, treat the organization as author:

Works Cited Entry	In-Text Citation
Commonwealth of Nations. *Drug Addiction*. Editis, 2004.	(Commonwealth 33)

- If organization is both author and publisher, skip the "Author" element and begin with the title of work:
  - List the organization as publisher:

Works Cited Entry	In-Text Citation
Pollution due to Urbanization. Houghton Mifflin Harcourt, 2009.	(*Pollution* 21)

Unknown Author

Simply skip the "Author" element:
- Begin with title of work:

Works Cited Entry	In-Text Citation
Yoga. Springer Nature, 1990.	(*Yoga* 45)

Edited

After the title of work, add:
- "Edited by" and
- The name of the editor in normal order ("first name last name" format):

Works Cited Entry	In-Text Citation
Lewis, Logan A. *The Funny Incident.* Edited by Madelyn Miller, HarperCollins. 2007.	(Lewis 29)

Translated

After the title of work, add:
- "Translated by" and
- The name of the translator in normal order ("first name last name" format):

Works Cited Entry	In-Text Citation
Clark, Dominic F. *A Visit to a Village.* Translated by Andrew Parker, Bonnier Books, 2009.	(Clark 22)

- In case you need to focus on the translation, start with the translator's name in the "Author" element:
  - Add the label "translator" after translator's name.
  - After the title of work, add "By" followed by the author's name:

Works Cited Entry	In-Text Citation
Patterson, Paisley, translator. *War on Drugs.* By Ivy Perry, Houghton Mifflin Harcourt, 2016.	(Patterson 22)

Chapter in a Book

Works Cited Entry	In-Text Citation
Henderson, Jaxon. "Corruption." *Global Terrorism*, Kodansha, 2014, pp. 334–49.	(Henderson 339)

Multivolume Set

Works Cited Entry	In-Text Citation
Johnson, Connor. *Balance Is Beneficial*. Penguin Random House, 2014. Vol. 6 of *Semantic Barriers in Peoples Communication English Language*.	(Johnson 329)

2+ Publishers

Works Cited Entry	In-Text Citation
Robinson, Alice. *Election System in India*. Hachette Livre / Oxford UP, 2008.	(Robinson 45)

E-Book

Works Cited Entry	In-Text Citation
Howard, Axel. *Republic Day Celebrations*. E-book ed., John Wiley & Sons, 2015.	(Howard 78)

Audiobook

Works Cited Entry	In-Text Citation
Foster, Nicholas. *Importance of Yoga*. Narrated by Leah Taylor, audiobook ed., unabridged ed., Mifflin Audiobooks, 2017.	(Foster 00:32:07–29)

6.3 Articles in Scholarly Journals

General Format:

Author's Last Name, First Name. "Article Title." *Publication Title*, vol.#, no.#, Date, pp. #–#.

Author's Last Name, First Name. "Article Title." *Publication Title*, vol.#, no.#, Date, URL or DOI.

- For the date of publication include day, month, and year (if known):
  - Remember to abbreviate the month if it has more than 4 letters.

Printed Journal

Works Cited Entry	In-Text Citation
Moore, Josiah. "Writing and Performance as Path." *Social Action*, vol. 3, no. 14, 2020, pp. 213–25.	(Moore 213)

Online Journal

Works Cited Entry	In-Text Citation
Stevenson, Amanda, et al. "The Impact of Contraceptive Access on High School Graduation." *Science Advances*, vol. 7, no. 19, 5 May 2021, https://advances.sciencemag.org/content/7/19/eabf6732.	(Stevenson et al. 22)

Special Issue

- Add the descriptor "special issue of" and insert the title of journal in italics:

Works Cited Entry	In-Text Citation
Simmons, Henry. "Agricultural Chemistry and Environment." *Green and Sustainable Chemistry*, special issue of *Journal of Biophysical Chemistry*, edited by Gabriella Clark, vol. 34, no. 7, 2021, pp. 45–67.	(Simmons 49)

In a Database (with a DOI)

Works Cited Entry	In-Text Citation
Ramirez, Madelyn. "School Uniforms." *Nature Communications*, vol. 45, no. 2, summer 2021, pp. 29–34. *AEBEL*, http://doi.org/1004.3548.5680/chkg77.	(Ramirez 29)

In a Database (with a URL)

Works Cited Entry	In-Text Citation
Phillips, Ezra B. "Penmanship and Calligraphy Samples." *ELife*, vol. 19, no. 5, Apr. 2020, pp. 124–35. *WorldCat*, www.worldcat.org/oclc/8288666345623.	(Phillips 124)

PDF of Online Journal

Works Cited Entry	In-Text Citation
Cooper, Andrew. "Modern Nonlinear Theory and Application." *Science Advances*, vol. 43, no. 7, 2018, pp. 221–34. *EBSCO*, ebsco.com/gfiles/408876459548. PDF download.	(Cooper 234)

6.4 Articles in Periodicals

General Format:

Author's Last Name, First Name. "Article Title." *Publication Title*, vol.#, no.#, Date, pp. #–#.

Author's Last Name, First Name. "Article Title." *Publication Title*, vol.#, no.#, Date, URL or DOI.

- For the date of publication include day, month, and year (if known):
  - Remember to abbreviate the month if it has more than 4 letters.

Printed Article in Newspaper

Works Cited Entry	In-Text Citation
Nelson, Bella. "Effects of Social Networking Sites." *The Washington Post*, 14 July 2020, pp. 19–21.	(Nelson 20)

- For a local newspaper, add the city of publication in square brackets if it is not included in the title of publication:

Works Cited Entry	In-Text Citation
Butler, Kinsley F. "A Railway Accident." *Transportation Technologies* [Indianapolis], 22 Oct. 1999, p. 39.	(Butler 39)

Online Article in Newspaper

Works Cited Entry	In-Text Citation
Parker, Claire. "Johnson Calls UK Crisis Talks as Sturgeon Says Another Scottish Independence Vote Is Inevitable." *The Washington Post*, 9 May 2021, www.washingtonpost.com/world/2021/05/09/scotland-independence-referendum-johnson-sturgeon/.	(Parker)

Printed Article in Magazine

Works Cited Entry	In-Text Citation
Russell, Harper A. "Behavioral and Brain Science." *Health*, vol. 16, no. 5, Jan. 2012, pp. 39–41.	(Russell 39)

Online Article in Magazine

Works Cited Entry	In-Text Citation
Mitchell, Samantha. "Mango Fruit." *Food and Nutrition*, vol. 14, no. 8, Apr. 2020, www.foodnnutrition.com/articles/fruit/305682705697.	(Mitchell)

Review

Works Cited Entry	In-Text Citation
Rodriguez, Jacob. Review of *Importance of Sleep*, by Matthew Powell. *International Journal of Medical Physics*, vol. 33, May 2018, pp. 216–29.	(Rodriguez 216)

6.5 Other Printed Works

General Format:

Author's Last Name, First Name. *Printed Work Title*. Publisher, Date, pp. #–#.

Published Interview

- Put the interviewee's name in the "Author" element:

Works Cited Entry	In-Text Citation
Campbell, Michael. *Interviews with Michael Campbell*. Conducted by Jack Flores, Pearson Education, 2018.	(Campbell)

Conference Proceedings

- Cite conference proceedings as a book:

Works Cited Entry	In-Text Citation
Jenkins, Thomas, et al., editors. *Proceedings of the Annual Meeting*. American Society of International Law, 2008.	(Jenkins et al. 2)

Lecture, Talk, and Speech

- Add the descriptor to specify the type of presentation:

Works Cited Entry	In-Text Citation
Cook, Gabriel. Lecture. Cubism in Arts, 16 May 2020, Chicago School of Arts.	(Cook)

Entry in Dictionary

Works Cited Entry	In-Text Citation
"Become, *V.* (2)." *Collins English Dictionary*, 8th ed., Scholastic, 2020, p. 175.	("Become" 175)

Entry in Encyclopedia

Works Cited Entry	In-Text Citation
"Frame." *Chambers Encyclopedia*, edited by Sofia Powell, 3rd ed., McGraw-Hill Education, 2001, p. 344.	("Frame" 344)

Dissertation and Theses

- Add labels "PhD dissertation," etc. to identify the document type:
  - If the dissertation was accessed online, include the database and URL in the second container:

Works Cited Entry	In-Text Citation
Brown, Sebastian. *Effective Ways of Reducing Air Pollution*. 2014. U of Toronto, PhD dissertation. *ProQuest*, search.proquest.com/docview/0783574542.	(Brown 18)

Short Story / Essay

Works Cited Entry	In-Text Citation
Richardson, Penelope. "The Lottery." *The Works of Penelope Richardson*, Oxford UP, 1999, pp. 122–31.	(Richardson 122)

Brochure

Works Cited Entry	In-Text Citation
New York. Trip Planner, 2014. Brochure.	(*New York* 4)

Letter

Works Cited Entry	In-Text Citation
Sanchez, Axel. Letter. *Great Love Stories: Love Letters*, 24 Sept. 2009, p. 16.	(Sanchez 16)

Report

Works Cited Entry	In-Text Citation
Young, David. *Etsy Report for Vintage Sellers 2018*. Etsy Publications, Feb. 2019.	(Young 11)

Executive Summary

Works Cited Entry	In-Text Citation
Executive summary. *How Expressive Arts Therapy and Outdoor Adventure Activities Can Increase Interpersonal Communication Skills: Adventure in Building Communication with Children,* Free Speech Association, 2015, www.freespeechassociation.com/article/title/2346564378476.	(Executive summary)

Poem

Works Cited Entry	In-Text Citation
Sanders, Eleanor. "Save Water Save Earth." *Collected Poems in English*, vol. 3, McGraw-Hill Education, 2005, p. 549.	(Sanders 549)

Play

Works Cited Entry	In-Text Citation
Reed, Michael. *Brave New World*, Cengage Learning, 2002, pp. 324–516.	(Reed 378)

Scripture

Works Cited Entry	In-Text Citation
The Koran. Translated by Muhammad Fahd, Oxford UP, 2018.	(*Koran*)

Bible

Works Cited Entry	In-Text Citation
The Bible. English Standard Version, Crossway, 2001.	(*Bible*, Ezek. 1.5)

6.6 Websites

General Format:

Author's Last Name, First Name. "Webpage Title." *Website Name*, Publisher (omit if same as website

name), Date, URL. Accessed Date.

Webpage

- Start with the author's name (if known):

Works Cited Entry	In-Text Citation
Edwards, Oliver. "Liberty is Not Anarchy." *Geomaterials*, 22 Oct. 2017, www.geomaterials.com/libertyisnotanarchy/. Accessed 11 May 2021.	(Edwards)

Wikipedia

Works Cited Entry	In-Text Citation
"Metabolism." *Wikipedia*, 5 May 2021, en.wikipedia.org/wiki/Metabolism. Accessed 21 May 2021.	("Metabolism")

Entire Website

Works Cited Entry	In-Text Citation
EDU. East Delta University, 26 Apr. 2021, www.eastdelta.edu.bd/.	(*EDU*)

Facebook

Works Cited Entry	In-Text Citation
Walker, Lucas. "Farewell Speech for Boss". *Facebook*, 19 May 2021, www.facebook.com/356875478560/.	(Walker)

Instagram

Works Cited Entry	In-Text Citation
Mitchell, Ryan. Photo of *Vogue* cover. *Instagram*, 28 Mar. 2021, www.instagram.com/p/Bdk_fB6FdkgqPw/.	(Mitchell)

Twitter

- If the author's nickname differs from the author's name, you may add the author's nickname in square brackets after the name:
  - Put the full text of tweet in double quotation marks with a sentence capitalization and a period at the end:

Works Cited Entry	In-Text Citation
Lopez, Victoria [@worlwidethinking_one]. "Cause Love's such an old fashioned word, and Love dares you to care for the people on the edge of the night." *Twitter*, 14 Sept. 2019, twitter.com/VictoriaLopez/status/2854734068723059867.	(Lopez)

Blog Post

Works Cited Entry	In-Text Citation
Baker, Carson. "Too Many Places: Overcoming The Paradox of Choice." *Nomadic Matt*, 6 May 2021, www.nomadicmatt.com/travel-blogs/how-to-deal-with-choice/.	(Baker)

6.7 Audiovisual Works

YouTube

- If the author is the same person who uploaded the video, skip the "Author" element and begin with the title of video:

Works Cited Entry	In-Text Citation
"Conversations on Time Management in English." *YouTube*, uploaded by Speak Confident English, 5 May 2021, www.youtube.com/watch?v=bASqSI559ZM.	("Conversations" 00:05:12–34)

- If the author is not the person who uploaded the video, start with the author's name:

Works Cited Entry	In-Text Citation
Peer, Marisa. "Do This to Completely Heal Your Body and Mind." *YouTube*, uploaded by Mindvalley Talks, 6 Sept. 2019, www.youtube.com/watch?v=egbiGhAiN8E.	(Peer 00:23:34–58)

TED Talk

Works Cited Entry	In-Text Citation
Nelson, Gabriel. "Meet the Women Fighting." *TED*, May 2015, www.ted.com/talks/gabriel_nelson_talks_about_women_fighting.	(Nelson)

Film

- Begin with the film title, followed by:
  - Name of the director,
  - Film studio or distributor,
  - Date of the release:

Works Cited Entry	In-Text Citation
Deep Breathing. Directed by Anthony Brooks, Sony Pictures, 2013.	(*Deep Breathing* 01:04:16–29)

TV Series

- Begin with the episode title (in quotation marks), followed by:
  - Series name in italics,
  - TV-show studio or distributor,
  - Date of the release:

Works Cited Entry	In-Text Citation
"Discrimination." *Relationships*, created by Isla Hall, season 1, episode 4, Universal, 3 Jan. 2018.	("Discrimination" 00:33:17–19)

Music Album

- Begin with the artist's name, followed by:
  - Album name in italics.
  - Record label:

Works Cited Entry	In-Text Citation
Cardigans. *Life*. Trampolene Records, 1995.	(Cardigans)

Song

- Begin with the artist's name, followed by:
  - Song title in quotation marks.
  - Album name in italics (if known).
  - Record label (if known).
  - Medium or URL of the retrieved song:

Works Cited Entry	In-Text Citation
Spears, Britney. "Toxic." *In the Zone*, Jive, 2003. *Spotify* app.	(Spears 00:02:21–29)

Podcast

Works Cited Entry	In-Text Citation
Phillips, Serenity M. "The Children of Morelia." Narrated by Phillips. *The New Yorker Radio Hour*, hosted by David Remnick, 23 Apr. 2021. *The New Yorker*, www.newyorker.com/podcast/the-new-yorker-radio-hour/the-children-of-morelia.	(Phillips 00:02:40–52)

Painting (in Museum)

- Begin with the artist's name, followed by:
    - Title of the painting in italics,
    - Date of creation,
    - Institution and city where the artwork is located:

Works Cited Entry	In-Text Citation
Scott, Dylan. *Pleasures of Gardening*. 1965, Museum of Fine Arts, Boston.	(Scott)

Photograph (Online)

- If you accessed the artwork online, add the date of artwork creation (NOT the date of publication on the website):

Works Cited Entry	In-Text Citation
Smith, Ariana. Photograph of *Taj Mahal*. "Entering the Taj Mahal at the Sunrise," by Smith, 11 Oct. 2013. *Visiting Center*, visitingcenter.com/titles/articles/7534742/.	(Smith)

Sculpture

- Begin with the artist's name, followed by:
    - Title of the sculpture in italics,
    - Date of creation,
    - Institution and city where the artwork is located,
    - Medium of the artwork:

Works Cited Entry	In-Text Citation
Michelangelo. *Pietà*. 1499, St. Peter's Basilica, Vatican City. Marble sculpture.	(Michelangelo)

Slides

Works Cited Entry	In-Text Citation
Picasso, Pablo. *Guernica.* 1937. Cubism in the Art, taught by Ryan Green, 18 Mar. 2021, School of the Art Institute of Chicago. Slide 18.	(Picasso, slide 18)

Table

Works Cited Entry	In-Text Citation
"Table 311.15: Number and Percentage of Students Enrolled in Degree-Granting Postsecondary Institutions, by Distance Education Participation, Location of Student, Level of Enrollment, and Control and Level of Institution: Fall 2018 and Fall 2019." *Digest of Education Statistics*, 2020, nces.ed.gov/programs/digest/d20/tables/dt20_311.15.asp.	("Table")

Chart

Works Cited Entry	In-Text Citation
Exchange Rates Graph for US Dollar and Indian Rupee. Vicking, 2018. Chart.	(*Exchange Rates Graph*)

Map

Works Cited Entry	In-Text Citation
Texas. Rand, 2016. Map.	(*Texas*)

6.8 Legal Works

For the legal works, treat the national government and agency as the organizational author:
- For congressional publications, include:
    - The number of the Congress,
    - The session of the hearing,
    - The number of the report.

Government Publication

Works Cited Entry	In-Text Citation
Ontario Ministry of Health. *Selected Findings from the Mental Health Supplement of the Ontario Health Survey.* Queen's Printer for Ontario, 1994.	(Ontario)

Resolution of International Convention

Works Cited Entry	In-Text Citation
United Nations, General Assembly. Convention on the Rights of the Child. Resolution 44/25, 20 Nov. 1989. *United Nations,* https://www.unicef.org/child-rights-convention. PDF download.	(United Nations)

US Supreme Court Decision

Works Cited Entry	In-Text Citation
United States, Supreme Court. *Gibbons v. Ogden.* vol. 231, 3 Aug. 1824, pp. 321–42. *Library of Congress,* https://tile.loc.gov/storage-services/service/dd/usgj/fnh9876/usrep347487	(United States)

US Code

Works Cited Entry	In-Text Citation
United States, Congress, House. United States Code. Title 12, section 298, Office of the Law Revision Counsel, 24 July 2018, uscode.house.gov.	(United States)

US Public Law

Works Cited Entry	In-Text Citation
United States, Congress. Public Law 124–134. *United States Statutes at Large*, vol. 214, 2014, pp. 2936–45. *U.S. Government Publishing Office*, www.gpo.gov/fhaag/pol/STATUTE-134/pdf/STATUTE-134.	(United States)

Federal Bill

Works Cited Entry	In-Text Citation
United States, Congress, House. To Combat Child Human Trafficking, and for Other Purposes. *Congress.gov*, www.congress.gov/bill/117th-congress/house-bill/3073?s=9&r=2. 117th Congress, 1st session, House Resolution 3073, introduced 7 May 2021.	(United States)

Executive Order

Works Cited Entry	In-Text Citation
United States, Executive Office of the President [George W. Bush]. Executive Order 11609: Delegating Certain Functions Vested in the President to Other Officers of the Government. 22 July 1971. *Federal Register*, vol. 1, no. 882, 1 Oct. 2004, pp. 7321–46, www.gpo.gov/fdsys/pkg/HY-0964337jvcd-997.pdf.	(United States)

State Senate Bill

Works Cited Entry	In-Text Citation
Wisconsin State, Legislature. Senate Bill 1. *Wisconsin State Legislature*, 5 Feb. 2020, docs.legis.wisconsin.gov/2019/related/proposals/jr0_sb1.	(Wisconsin State)

Treaty

Works Cited Entry	In-Text Citation
United States, Senate. Agricultural Commodities Agreement. *Congress.gov*, www.congress.gov/995/cnhc/documents98/ACA-864hgf997.pdf. Treaty between the United States and the Philippines.	(United States)

Constitution

Works Cited Entry	In-Text Citation
The Constitution of the United States: A Transcription. National Archives, U.S. National Archives and Records Administration, 28 Feb. 2017, www.archives.gov/founding-docs/constitution-transcript.	(*Constitution*)

6.9 Personal Communications

General Format:

Author's Last Name, First Name. Kind of communication with the author. Date.

- When documenting a personal communication, reference to yourself:
    - As "author," or
    - By your name.

Personal Communication

Works Cited Entry	In-Text Citation
Nelson, Benjamin. Personal communication with author. 15 May 2021.	(Nelson)

Personal Interview

- Personal interviews are interviews that you have conducted yourself:
    - Treat the name of the interviewee as the author's name:

Works Cited Entry	In-Text Citation
Jenkins, Ella. E-mail interview with the author, 12 Mar. 2020.	(Jenkins)
Ward, Mila. Telephone interview with the author. 22 July 2020.	(Ward)

Letter

Works Cited Entry	In-Text Citation
Patterson, Mateo. Letter to the author. 17 May 2021. Typescript.	(Patterson)

E-mail

Works Cited Entry	In-Text Citation
Bell, Scarlett. E-mail to the author. 12 Apr. 2021.	(Bell)

Classroom Material

Works Cited Entry	In-Text Citation
Syllabus for The Civil Rights Movement and the Effects. Taught by Daniel Parker, winter 2020, Princeton U, Philadelphia.	(Syllabus 131)

7.0 MLA SAMPLE PAPER

For the purpose of demonstrating a general layout and formatting (such as formatting of in-text citations, Works Cited list, tables and figures, title page, headings, notes, lists, etc.), the following MLA sample paper contains non-relative Works Cited list entries that do not match in-text citations in the paper.
In a real paper, all in-text citations should match Works Cited list entries and vice versa.

White 1

Andrew J. White

Professor Richardson

English 2210

20 April 2021

Literacy Essentials

Lorem ipsum dolor sit amet, consectetur adipiscing elit. Phasellus lorem nulla, fermentum a aliquam sed. Donec aliquet tempor nisi nec sagittis. Praesent tincidunt augue massa, ut maximus eros tincidunt sit amet. Nullam consequat venenatis ligula, vitae blandit tellus. Nullam dapibus quam nec tellus lacinia viverra (Jackson and Brooks 229). Mauris lacus magna, pulvinar vitae non, maximus ac odio. In vestibulum nisl non libero, quis ultricies ex venenatis. Conversation questions for dreams, daydreams and nightmares offered for students of the ESL classroom:

Do you dream regularly?

What is a daydream?

What is your worst nightmare?

What is the difference between our daydreams and our dreams at night?

What is the difference between our everyday life and dreaming while we are sleeping?

Global Warming

Quisque ac quam ut magna cursus sollicitudin. Maecenas ultrices nec mi non vulputate. Fusce elementum egestas leo vitae vehicula. Maecenas at convallis orci. Integer convallis ipsum at pulvinar imperdiet. Suspendisse potenti (*Live Art*). Maecenas orci sit amet molestie lobortis. Proin at feugiat magna. In feugiat dolor vel nulla aliquet blandit sed quis metus. Phasellus lobortis elit non arcu finibus sed pulvinar turpis, eget hendrerit urna. Mauris scelerisque nec leo at vehicula purus pharetra eleifend auris viverra a massa eget consectetur. Integer et neque vel lacus gravida finibus et molestie lobortis ullamcorper eu vitae diam. Phasellus ornare dui ut mi consequat ultricies. Donec vestibulum purus et vulputate vulputate (Executive summary). Vivamus in urna quam, consectetur eget tristique ut, fermentum eget sem. Mauris consequat magna ac tortor sodales nisi vel quam.

Environment

Donec libero tortor, vestibulum non lobortis ut, aliquet eget nisi. Nulla rutrum tortor id orci lobortis ultricies ("Metabolism"). Mauris viverra a massa eget consectetur. Integer et neque vel lacus gravida finibus et at ante. Cras non hendrerit ante, semper mollis lectus. Aenean aliquet ornare varius. Cras nulla sapien, posuere at massa quis, tincidunt tempus dui. Nunc auctor ultricies luctus. Praesent tincidunt augue massa, ut maximus eros tincidunt sit amet.

Table 1

Number and Percentage of Students Enrolled in Degree-Granting Postsecondary Institutions[a]

Institution	Number of Students	Percent of Students
Public	14,539,257	65.9
Private	5,112,155	61.3
Nonprofit	4,131,846	69.6
For-profit	980,309	26.6

Adapted from: U.S. Department of Education. *Digest of Education Statistics,* 2020, table 311.15, nces.ed.gov/programs/digest/d20/tables/dt20_311.15.asp.

a. These figures include data for fall 2018 of the 50 states and the District of Columbia and exclude data for fall 2019 and for undergraduate and postbaccalaureate institutions.

Nullam consequat venenatis ligula, vitae blandit tellus. Nullam dapibus quam nec tellus lacinia viverra. Mauris lacus magna, pulvinar vitae sagittis non, maximus ac odio. In vestibulum nisl non libero commodo, quis ultricies ex venenatis. Sed egestas fermentum dignissim. Sed massa lectus, egestas sit amet tincidunt eget, rhoncus non mi. Mauris rutrum libero ante, id porta velit sagittis finibus. Aliquam

sollicitudin quam eget ex, vel ullamcorper quam mollis. Integer eros massa, maximus in eleifend non,

porttitor quis eros ("Discrimination" 00:03:19–34).

Wildlife

Sed nisi arcu, dignissim nec justo id, lacinia tincidunt dolor. Proin sed tempor nulla, a sagittis

nulla. Maecenas eget nisl et odio tempus egestas in et lacus. Quisque fermentum egestas sem. Phasellus

urna quam, consectetur eget tristique ut, fermentum eget sem (*New York*). Mauris consequat magna ac

tortor placerat in nec enim. Praesent massa, ut maximus eros tincidunt sit amet.

Fig. 1. Lawren Harris. *Mountain Forms*. 1926, Museum London.

Nullam consequat venenatis ligula, vitae blandit tellus. Nullam quam nec tellus lacinia viverra.

Mauris lacus magna, vitae sagittis non, maximus ac odio. In vestibulum nisl non libero commodo, quis

ultricies ex venenatis (Picasso, slide 18). Vivamus libero turpis, eu placerat ut, porta ac turpis. Morbi

lobortis neque vitae ex tincidunt, et rhoncus purus placerat. Quisque nisi est, dapibus in sagittis non,

cursus quis odio. Donec a vehicula tortor. Mauris purus magna, dapibus eget finibus tempor, varius

sollicitudin quam eget ex condimentum, vel ullamcorper quam mollis. Integer eros massa, maximus in eget magna. Suspendisse pretium sollicitudin orci sed ultrices. Proin at laoreet lacus. Nunc quis accumsan tortor vehicula purus pharetra eleifend auctor.

Flora

Phasellus et fermentum neque. Ut semper arcu arcu, sit amet laoreet sem porttitor sit amet. Morbi sed mauris neque (Cooper 221–32). Sed ac orci felis. Pellentesque morbi tristique senectus et netus et malesuada fames ac turpis egestas. Nulla facilisi. Pellentesque dapibus tellus at nunc efficitur, ac vehicula ante ultricies. Liu summarises the main assumption underlying CPTED[1] — namely, that a modification of the physical environment can lead to a reduction in the crime rate. The work focuses on applying approved and tested CPTED strategies to the renewal of urban habitats.[2] The physical causes "lead to increased crime and fear of crime."[3]

Nullam eu eleifend est. In tortor est, faucibus quis justo non, faucibus venenatis nulla. Sed ut semper neque. Etiam vel tortor sed leo sollicitudin accumsan. Curabitur bibendum justo nulla, non ornare tortor laoreet. Vestibulum odio ligula, mattis sit amet odio (Syllabus).

Fauna

Mauris tempor id tortor id scelerisque. Praesent mattis justo eget augue ornare, eget tempus augue auctor. Class aptent taciti sociosqu ad litora torquent per conubia nostra, per inceptos himenaeos. Praesent vitae commodo urna (Brown 23). Fusce metus libero, luctus vitae tempor id, lacinia posuere magna. Phasellus tempus eleifend elit at varius. Suspendisse quis nisi sed ante luctus. Phasellus sollicitudin orci in suscipit, sit amet accumsan nisi condimentum. Mauris accumsan gravida sollicitudin. Fusce metus ligula, malesuada quis tellus vel, sagittis interdum leo. Nulla egestas pulvinar tellus. Praesent ultricies magna vel imperdiet dapibus.

Air Pollution

Donec eget luctus ipsum. Suspendisse potenti. Sed tortor tortor, blandit eget tristique quis, rutrum nec tortor. Morbi scelerisque in mi nec pulvinar. Nunc sit amet ipsum vel eros tincidunt volutpat. Ut ac dolor aliquam, efficitur erat vel, malesuada velit. Nulla vitae nisl sit amet nulla sodales convallis ut sit amet diam. Vivamus quis quam massa. Nulla ultrices dolor faucibus nisl mollis, vitae tincidunt est egestas (Commonwealth). Fusce vitae tellus, sit amet finibus lectus. Aenean finibus porttitor volutpat. Accessibility and convenience:

1. the broad variety of products and services;

2. online comparison;

3. adequate buildings;

4. basic and urban infrastructure services;

5. proffered location;

6. public amenities;

7. centralized and smart home system; and

8. comfort and security.

Quisque sollicitudin, mauris id scelerisque sollicitudin, ante lorem tempor tellus, a tincidunt felis tortor dictum enim. Curabitur scelerisque quam sem, et auctor mi ultrices in. Suspendisse potenti. Phasellus iaculis faucibus ligula, egestas feugiat felis sodales nec.

Ex. 1. Abel Korzeniowski, Evgeni's Waltz.

Nullam consequat venenatis ligula, vitae blandit tellus. Nullam dapibus quam nec tellus lacinia viverra. Mauris lacus magna, pulvinar vitae sagittis non, maximus ac odio. In vestibulum nisl non libero commodo, quis ultricies ex venenatis. Sed ullamcorper vestibulum tortor, vitae mollis leo. Maecenas gravida tellus ut lacus maximus, in rhoncus dolor dapibus. Nunc rhoncus posuere dui, vitae euismod arcu convallis et. Mauris vestibulum dolor aliquet, semper lorem in, congue enim. Aliquam pulvinar sit amet ligula eu tincidunt. Ut ut quam accumsan, iaculis mauris eleifend, cursus diam. Donec ut libero venenatis, ultrices diam sit amet, dictum tellus. Vestibulum ante ipsum primis in faucibus orci luctus et ultrices posuere cubilia curae; Maecenas feugiat tincidunt orci nec vulputate. Etiam lobortis et erat sodales convallis (Stevenson et al.).

Etiam est nunc, dignissim quis leo eu, ornare rutrum enim. Pellentesque porta interdum magna, quis finibus justo elementum lacinia. In auctor, enim non volutpat ultricies, erat eros ullamcorper urna, eu faucibus leo libero quis enim. Maecenas facilisis risus eget velit dictum, in accumsan ex venenatis. Duis gravida lacinia ex sit amet bibendum. Nunc vel nisl turpis ("Become" 175). Vestibulum facilisis turpis vitae magna egestas faucibus. Proin interdum id erat vel eleifend. Mauris volutpat porttitor enim, eget ultrices libero mollis vel. Mauris mattis sapien et sem tristique lacinia. Mauris lobortis mauris ac ornare laoreet. Integer a neque ut turpis dapibus varius id et ex.

In non urna elementum, aliquet magna vel, interdum ex. Sed vehicula congue ipsum, ac cursus libero aliquam et. In augue risus, fermentum nec mi a, eleifend efficitur massa. Cras pellentesque nulla quis laoreet mattis. Vivamus hendrerit efficitur diam, non ullamcorper turpis euismod id. Aliquam a mauris id metus condimentum ultrices nec ut diam. Praesent quis risus id tellus tincidunt suscipit.

Endnotes

[1] Liu uses their own theory based on the crime rate relation (235).

[2] See Liu 235.

[2] See Liu 236.

Works Cited

Brown, Sebastian. *Effective Ways of Reducing Air Pollution*. 2014. U of Toronto, PhD dissertation.

    ProQuest, search.proquest.com/docview/0783574542.

"Become, *V.* (2)." *Collins English Dictionary*, 8th ed., Scholastic, 2020, p. 175.

Campbell, Michael. *Interviews with Michael Campbell*. Conducted by Jack Flores, Pearson Education,

    2018.

Clark, Dominic F. *A Visit to a Village*. Translated by Andrew Parker, Bonnier Books, 2009.

Commonwealth of Nations. *Drug Addiction*. Editis, 2004.

Cook, Gabriel. Lecture. Cubism in Arts, 16 May 2020, Chicago School of Arts.

Cooper, Andrew. "Modern Nonlinear Theory and Application." *Science Advances*, vol. 43, no. 7, 2018,

    pp. 221–34. *EBSCO*, ebsco.com/gfiles/408876459548. PDF download.

"Discrimination." *Relationships*, created by Isla Hall, season 1, episode 4, Universal, 3 Jan. 2018.

Executive summary. *How Expressive Arts Therapy and Outdoor Adventure Activities Can Increase*

    Interpersonal Communication Skills: Adventure in Building Communication with Children,

    Free Speech Association, 2015,

"First Day in College." *The Students Association Weekly Newsletter*, Students Association, 14 Mar.

    2021. E-mail.

Garcia, Savannah. *A Surprise Birthday Party: When the Last Bell Goes*. HarperCollins, 2018.

Henderson, Jaxon. "Corruption." *Global Terrorism*, Kodansha, 2014, pp. 334–49.

Howard, Axel. *Republic Day Celebrations*. E-book ed., John Wiley & Sons, 2015.

Jackson, Addison, and Santiago Brooks. *A Journey in an Overcrowded Bus*. Scholastic, 2021.

Live Art: The Awakened Performer. 24 Feb.–5 Mar. 2017, Museum of Fine Arts, Boston.

Madonna. *Rebel Heart Tour*. 23 Jan. 2016, American Airlines Arena, Miami.

"Metabolism." *Wikipedia*, 5 May 2021, en.wikipedia.org/wiki/Metabolism. Accessed 21 May 2021.

Michelangelo. *Pietà*. 1499, St. Peter's Basilica, Vatican City. Marble sculpture.

Mitchell, Ryan. Photo of *Vogue* cover. *Instagram*, 28 Mar. 2021,

    www.instagram.com/p/Bdk_fB6FdkgqPw/.

Moore, Josiah. "Writing and Performance as Path." *Social Action*, vol. 3, no. 14, 2020, pp. 213–25.

Nelson, Benjamin. Personal communication with author. 15 May 2021.

Nelson, Gabriel. "Meet the Women Fighting." *TED*, May 2015,

    www.ted.com/talks/gabriel_nelson_talks_about_women_fighting.

New York. Trip Planner, 2014. Brochure.

Peer, Marisa. "Do This to Completely Heal Your Body and Mind." *YouTube*, uploaded by Mindvalley

    Talks, 6 Sept. 2019, www.youtube.com/watch?v=egbiGhAiN8E.

———. "Immune Based Therapies, Vaccines and Antimicrobials." *Food and Nutrition Sciences*, vol. 6,

    no. 14, Jan. 2021, p. 44. *AEBEL*, http://doi.org/1004.3548.5680/chkg77.

Picasso, Pablo. *Guernica*. 1937. Cubism in the Art, taught by Ryan Green, 18 Mar. 2021, School of the

    Art Institute of Chicago. Slide 18.

Pollution due to Urbanization. Houghton Mifflin Harcourt, 2009.

Spears, Britney. "Toxic." *In the Zone*, Jive, 2003. *Spotify* app.

Stevenson, Amanda, et al. "The Impact of Contraceptive Access on High School Graduation." *Science

    Advances*, vol. 7, no. 19, 5 May 2021, https://advances.sciencemag.org/content/7/19/eabf6732.

Syllabus for The Civil Rights Movement and the Effects. Taught by Daniel Parker, winter 2020,

    Princeton U, Philadelphia.

The Bible. English Standard Version, Crossway, 2001.

United States, Supreme Court. *Gibbons v. Ogden*. vol. 231, 3 Aug. 1824, pp. 321–42. *Library of

    Congress*, https://tile.loc.gov/storage-services/service/dd/usgj/fnh9876/usrep347487.

Ward, Mila. Telephone interview with the author. 22 July 2020.

SOURCES

Since the 9th edition of the MLA handbook is a new release, there are fewer supplementary resources than for the previous 8th edition.

For detailed MLA standards and procedures, please consult the *MLA Handbook 9th Edition*:
- o ISBN-10: 1603293515
- o ISBN-13: 978-1603293518

The Online Modern Language Association Style Center offers resources to support the use of the *MLA Handbook 9th Edition* available at https://style.mla.org

Additional Print Resources

- The MLA Guide to Digital Literacy, by Ellen C. Carillo:
  - o ISBN-13: 978-1603294393
  - o ISBN-10: 1603294392
- The MLA Guide to Undergraduate Research in Literature, by Elizabeth Brookbank and H. Faye Christenberry:
  - o ISBN-13: 978-1603294362
  - o ISBN-10: 1603294368

Other supplemental resources can be found at https://mla.org/books

In case you are using MLA style for a class assignment, please counsel your instructor for assistance with using MLA style.

Your instructor is the final authority on how to properly apply MLA style guidelines in your specific case.

FREE **MLA "In-Text Citations & Works Cited" Tables** from the author are available at:
https://appearancepublishers.wordpress.com/mla-9-simplified/

MORE FROM THE AUTHOR

CHECK MORE BOOKS
on Amazon

https://www.amazon.com/Appearance-Publishers/e/B091TLWPW9

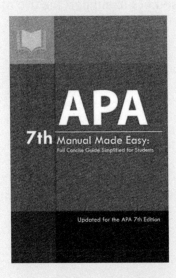

APA 7th Manual Made Easy

MLA Handbook 9th Edition Simplified

https://www.amazon.com/gp/product/B091SMVWKN/

https://www.amazon.com/gp/product/B092MY8YWT/

**APA 7th Quick Study
Guidelines in Tables**

**Strong Verbs Thesaurus
for Fiction Writers**

https://www.amazon.com/gp/product/B0938D4QR4

https://www.amazon.com/gp/product/B0933KSDSD